D0395698

PENGUIN BOOKS

THE TAO JONES AVERAGES

Bennett W. Goodspeed, who had overcome the handicaps of having an MBA and working for several prominent Wall Street firms, was a student of Oriental philosophy, a frequent lecturer, and a publisher of articles about man's bicameral mind. In addition, he was a founder of Inferential Focus, a New York-based consulting firm that develops intelligence by regularly absorbing information from more than 200 publications. Accordingly, this firm advises 75 clients—which include the White House, professional investment firms, and Fortune 500 companies—about changing economic and social trends.

THE TAO JONES AVERAGES
A Guide to Whole-Brained Investing

Bennett W. Goodspeed

PENGUIN BOOKS

PENGUIN BOOKS
Published by the Penguin Group
Viking Penguin, a division of Penguin Books USA Inc.,
375 Hudson Street, New York, New York 10014, U.S.A.
Penguin Books Ltd, 27 Wrights Lane,
London W8 5TZ, England
Penguin Books Australia Ltd., Ringwood,
Victoria, Australia
Penguin Books Canada Ltd, 10 Alcorn Avenue, Suite 300,
Toronto, Ontario, Canada M4V 3B2
Penguin Books (N.Z.) Ltd, 182–190 Wairau Road,
Auckland 10, New Zealand

Penguin Books Ltd, Registered Offices:
Harmondsworth, Middlesex, England

First published in the United States of America by
E.P. Dutton, Inc., 1983
Published by Viking Penguin Inc. 1984

7 9 10 8 6

LIBRARY OF CONGRESS CATALOGING IN PUBLICATION DATA
Goodspeed, Bennett W.
    The Tao-Jones averages.
    1. Investments.   2. Investment analysis.   3. Tao.
I. Title.
HG4521.G56   1984   332.6'78   84-11015
ISBN 0 14 00.7368 X

Printed in the United States of America
Set in Palatino

*Dedicated to
everyone who has the guts
to follow his gut*

CONTENTS

PREFACE

"We have a whole staff of experts who are supposed to keep track of changing trends. So why do we need you?" Such comments were typical of those I received from businesses in 1975, when I first started marketing a business inferential service, a service that specialized in intuitively identifying changing business conditions.

By relying on the experts of opinion and numerical spreadsheets, businessmen and investors all too often were taken by surprise when conditions changed, because they analyzed rather than *saw* the world around them. I was

unable to make this point successfully until one of my partners, Joe Kelly, sent me an article about the two sides of our
brains, which, although they look alike, operate very differ-
ently.

I began explaining our inference service by pointing out
that experts are specialized thinkers who have developed
the analytic, deductive skills of their left hemispheres.
Changing conditions, however, could not be analyzed until
after the fact. Thus, the visual, intuitive, and sensing
qualities of the right hemisphere, missing from the thinking
of most experts, were necessary to sense change in the early
stages. By reading over 150 publications on a regular basis,
our firm was frequently able to show clients where change
was beginning to happen long before it could be measured
by the numbers.

This distinction proved effective, and our company, Inferential Focus, entered an era of dynamic growth. In turn, I
began to read all the articles I could find on the nature of the
bicameral mind. In addition, I formed the Right Hemisphere Club to exchange information on a network basis
with others interested in the field. The insights I gained not
only helped our company grow, but also afforded me the
opportunity to view myself and others in a different light.

After I read *The Tao of Pooh* by Benjamin Hoff, I became
interested in the Chinese philosophy of Taoism (pronounced Dowism). This marvelous little book explains the
concept of Taoism through an examination of A. A. Milne's
familiar characters. On further study of Taoism, I became
fascinated by the strong resemblance between what Lao
Tsu, Taoism's founder, advocated—and the characteristics of
the right side of the brain that have been discovered by
modern science only recently—some 2,500 years after Lao
Tsu's death.

Fate then played its hand. At a seminar run by Tony Buzan, author of *The Brain User's Guide*, I met Bill Whitehead. When I discovered that Bill was an editor at Dutton, I remarked how much I enjoyed their book, *The Tao of Pooh*, and went on to suggest that his publishing house consider a book call *The Tao* (pronounced Dow) *Jones Averages*.

Two weeks later Bill called my office to tell me that he had been thinking about *The Tao Jones Averages* idea, and felt it was something he'd like to publish. Furthermore, Bill wondered, would I write the book?

Once I said yes, the horror of my commitment to do something I had never done before set in. Things were not made any easier by the fact that I had agreed to finish the book within four months.

I made my deadline, and in the process learned a great deal about myself. I was frequently helped by Lao Tsu's advice, including "Let the mind go where it will."

While writing the book, my mind seemed to go in the damndest directions—often taking courses seemingly opposite to my writing plans. At first I found this to be very disconcerting.

Learning to go with the mind's "flow" was much like letting loose a horse's reins while riding, secure in the faith that the horse would know its way back to the barn even if I didn't. When I had gained confidence in my mind's ability, I was continually amazed at the directions and journeys on which it took me. I was even more amazed at how pertinent these destinations turned out to be in the creation of this book.

As Lao Tsu states, "There is no greater evil than forcing others to change." In like fashion, *The Tao Jones Averages* is not meant to be another "how-to" book. Rather, it should be viewed as being like a shoe store, where the reader is invited to take with him or her what fits.

The translation of the *Tao Te Ching* that I have used in this book is by Archie J. Bahm, Professor of Philosophy, University of New Mexico (Frederick Ungar Publishing Co., N.Y.). There are many translations of Lao Tsu's work (it is the most heavily translated book in English, with the exception of the Bible), and these translations tend to be at considerable variance. I chose Bahm's because, unlike most, it concentrated on Lao Tsu's message rather than his poetry. In short, I found it to be the most direct, modern, and practical of all the translations I reviewed.

THE TAO JONES AVERAGES
A Guide to Whole-Brained Investing

1

THE STREET WHERE YOUR MONEY LIVES

Nature's way is simple and easy, but men prefer the intricate and artificial.
—LAO TSU

If you don't know who you are, the stock market is an expensive place to find out.
—ADAM SMITH,
   The Money Game

The United States stock market was founded on May 17, 1792, with the signing of the Buttonwood Agreement and the start of trading of company certificates of ownership. In the ensuing years, as a repository of funds from wealthy individuals, the stock market helped finance the railroads and steel companies, and thus contributed to America's early era of dynamic industrial growth.

In the 1920s the general public first discovered the "game" and its easy money. As a result, the twenties turned into a decade of excess that ended with the economically and emotionally disastrous crash of 1929. Investment theories abounded even before the twenties, and flourished until the early 1960s. Investing, however, remained more or less an art until 1963, when Donaldson, Lufkin, and Jenrette published the first "scientific" research report.

This 38-page report on Burlington Industries, a leading textile firm, hit a responsive chord within the professional investment community, and things have never been quite the same since. With the exception of the '29 crash, this first Burlington Industries report may be the most significant event in Wall Street's history. It symbolized the start of a shift toward scientific fundamentalism, whereby security analysis would become dominated by "the best and the brightest," people who specialized in following the trends in just one industry.

Security analysis is so glorified on Wall Street today that each year *Institutional Investor* magazine polls professional money managers to find out what analysts are considered to be the best. The top three picks are then honored by the magazine by being elected members of their "All-Star Research Team." Egos are further boosted when caricatures of the winners in football uniforms are depicted on the magazine's cover (never has a football team had so many players with spectacles).

With such brilliant specialists (many of whom are paid between $200,000 and $500,000 per year) analyzing the Fortune 500 and other companies and reporting their recommendations to investment institutions such as banks, insurance companies, and investment advisers, what chance does an individual investor have of competing in the market? How can one win when institutional investors not only control 50 percent of stock equity ownership and over

70 percent of the volume of shares traded on the N.Y. Stock Exchange, but also have access to the information compiled by such brilliant analytic scholars? Logically speaking, it doesn't make sense for individuals to play the market.

Well, there is bad news and good news: If we are the pioneers in the wagon train, we must face the fact that the cavalry isn't coming to save us—but don't despair, for there aren't any Indians! Most individual investors cannot gain proper access to sophisticated institutional research. But don't worry, *because it doesn't work!* The pros are not beating the market; *it* is beating *them!*

Consider the results. Over the last fifteen years through 1982 only 32 percent of the professional money managers have performed as well as or better than the stock market averages. Furthermore, according to A. G. Becker Fund Evaluation Service, only 17 percent of these managers outperformed inflation! If 100 typical money managers were graded as if they were in a school class, only 17 would get A's, B's, or C's, whereas the other 83 would get D's and F's!

Why do investment professionals get such poor marks? The main reason is that they are victims of their own methodology. By making a science out of an art, they are opting to be precisely wrong rather than generally correct. By creating the illusion of certainty where there is none, analysts are continually surprised by changing conditions. As Mitzi Malevich, a senior investment officer of the St. Paul Companies, states, "Next to Congress, Wall Street analysts are the greatest lagging indicator around." Like the message tape in "Mission Impossible," they tend to self-destruct. The "pros" are just not keeping up with "the Joneses"—that is, with the Dow Jones Averages.

To get a feel for how this can happen and how we can

benefit from Wall Street's loser's game, we need to look at the basic philosophies used in investing in the market: fundamental, technical, contrary opinion, and random walk (indexing).

Fundamental analysis, which is the most prevalent mode practiced by professional investors, operates on the assumption that all stocks have inherent, determinable values that are often incorrectly appraised in the marketplace. By identifying these discrepancies, fundamentalists feel, an investor can achieve a winning performance record.

The technical approach is predicated on the belief that the market does work "perfectly," that all known fundamental and factual information about a company is automatically reflected in the price of the stock. In this view, the fundamental method is pointless, since the market is "all-knowing." The key to making money in the technical approach, therefore, is to spot patterns that indicate supply and demand changes. In the Dow theory, first developed in 1908, technical analysts have coined a whole phraseology of their own, such as "support levels," "flags," "bottoms and tops," "relative strength," and "head and shoulders" (which is not a brand of shampoo). Like the fundamental approach, technical analysis also has a good news/bad news situation. For the individual investor, the good news is that technical analytic advice from the best-known professionals is available to the public at an affordable price; the bad news is that, over time, this advice hasn't worked (at least statistical measurements have not yet validated its effectiveness).

Random walkers and contrarian investors both feel that neither the fundamental nor the technical approach works. Since the market is unpredictable, random walkers argue, one cannot add value to investment decision-making. This philosophy has contributed to the growth of "index funds," which are pools of money "indexed" so that they will duplicate the stock averages. The object of "indexed money" is not to beat the averages (whichever one it happens to be tied to—usually the S&P 500), but to maintain a similar performance.

Contrarians, on the other hand, feel that fundamental and technical information tends to create consensus values that frequently are grossly mistaken. Contrarians love to tell the story about the 1970 *Institutional Investor*'s annual conference, at which 2,000 of the nation's top money managers picked the "stock of the year." Their choice? National Student Marketing, which promptly declined from $140 per share to $7 within just five months. Consequently, the contrarians feel that all one has to do to win in the market is to bet against the popular investment trends—so to speak, bettings against "Houses" (the Wall Street "houses").

THE NATURE OF THE MARKET
VERSUS FUNDAMENTAL ANALYSIS

Wall Street does not seem to have figured out what Mr. Edward C. Johnson, Jr., of Fidelity Management, the now retired "dean of Wall Street," understood when he said, "I have been absorbed and immersed since 1924 in the market and I know this is no science. It is an art form. . . . It is a personal intuition, sensing patterns of behavior." Yet despite the fact that the market is famous for its fickle, crowdlike behavior, the Street's research analysts keep applying rules of logic and formula thinking. Behaving like the fanatic (one who, when he loses sight of his goals, redoubles his efforts), they apply logic to an illogical game. By applying male (yang) logic to the market's female (yin-type) behavior, professional investors are often guilty of what Lao Tsu referred to as "trying to understand running water by catching it in a bucket."

A herd is a synonym for a crowd, and as John Train states in *Dance of the Money Bees*, "The herd instinct seems to be the strongest human emotion, one that the race is constantly breeding off as the mavericks are liquidated. Happiness is running with the crowd." Gustave Le Bon's book, *The Crowd*, still considered by many to be the most definitive work on mass psychology despite its 1895 publishing date, explains how a crowd goes from controlled logic to uncontrolled emotion, resulting in conscious personalities vanishing into a collective mind. The crowd, as opposed to the individual, possesses the spontaneity, violence, ferocity, and heroics of primitive beings.

If you have been wondering about the success of Wall Street analysts' scientific, logical, fundamental approach to coping with crowd behavior, you're not alone. It is fair to say that the disenchantment with institutional research is reaching epidemic proportions, and the record shows why: It is illogical to treat the market logically.

The fundamental approach to security analysis, though its popularization started in 1963 with the Burlington Industries report, actually began in 1934 when Graham and Dodd published *Security Analysis*, a 778-page bible for the scientific study of corporations. This book, which contains 178 pages on financial measurements, is...well, boring. It has nonetheless been through three editions, and can be found on the bookshelves of most security analysts. Graham and Dodd believed that each stock has an inherent value based on its earnings power (earnings-per-share ÷ price = price-earnings ratio) which can be determined by carefully following the economy, the company's industry, and the company itself. Sounds simple enough, but as Casey Stengel said, "Knowing how to do something and doing it are two different things."

One of the requirements of fundamental analysis is understanding the economy. This task is not easy, as Paul Samuelson, the author of the most widely read text on economics, admitted. When asked to predict next year's economic trends, he refused, stating, "To be published is to be found out." The fallibility of economists has spawned many jokes such as the one about a doctor, an architect, and an economist who were debating what was the world's oldest profession. The doctor claimed that his was the oldest, as God performed surgery by removing Adam's rib. The architect countered by pointing out that God practiced architecture by designing the universe from chaos. After a pause, the economist asked, "Who do you think created the chaos?"

Another requirement of fundamental analysis is to follow industry trends. This task is also very difficult, since corporate managers themselves are often surprised by unforeseen events, as the recent history of Detroit sadly reveals. If company management cannot predict its earnings, how can an outside analyst be expected to succeed? And even when earning projections are right on target, the company's stocks often do not respond as predicted. In fact, the fundamental, analytic method has many shortcomings.

1) One cannot analyze events until they have already happened. Numbers, the "oxygen" of analysis, lag behind reality. Analytic methodology is ineffective in identifying

change in the early stages and thus contributes to what Marshall McLuhan refers to as man's tendency to walk into the future looking in the rearview mirror.

2) Analysis can be equated with poker. Security analysts carefully follow the table talk of the game (what company management will publicly state about its business) and examine the upcards (corporate history and published statistics). Although analysts effectively follow and communicate these two aspects of the game, they either ignore or ineffectively guess at the other major element—the downcards (what management is not saying or what is unknown). Why? Because their training and tools are ineffective in dealing with nonquantifiable, "soft" data. This data is comparable to the dark side of the moon in the astronomy of yore. On Wall Street what is known tends to get glorified at the expense of the unknown.

3) In their frenzied activity, analysts create an overload of information. It is not uncommon to see the desk of institutional money managers filled with stacks of research reports. On Monday morning, these stacks often run two feet high! One portfolio manager keeps up with the overload by keeping *two* full-size trash baskets in his office. It is very easy for the professional money manager to mistake activity for effectiveness as he plows through his daily paper snowstorm.

4) Since analysts talk to the same corporate managers and to each other, and look at the same statistics, it is no wonder that they have a tendency to reach similar conclusions. This in turn tends to lull professional investors into a false sense of security through consensus forecasts. Their mathematical complexities tend to provide a false feeling of scientific precision. As E. F. Schumacher said in 1961,

"Make a guess, call it an assumption, and derive an estimate by subtle calculation. The estimate is then presented as a result of scientific reasoning, something far superior to mere guesswork. Colossal planning errors result because the method offers a bogus answer where the entrepreneurial judgement is required."

5) By specializing in just one industry, analysts are prone to be surprised by developments outside their focus, just as, say, the Swiss watch industry was unprepared for developments in the semiconductor field. Predictions are often in error not as to what is analyzed, but as to what is *not* taken into account.

Despite the limitations of their methodology, the All-Star team of security analysts continues to exert a powerful influence on Wall Street. Why? One reason is the undeniable fact that, even though analysts' opinions often do not reflect reality, they still have the power in the short run to influence stock prices up and down. Also, their opinions fulfill a psychological need of professional managers by making uncertainty appear to be more certain. However, the biggest irony of all is the urging of in-house lawyers and administrative bureaucrats for their money managers to follow the "prudent man rule," which in effect requires that money managers do what other men of prudence are doing. Managers are thus encouraged, even coerced, to join with the lemmings as they march toward the sea cliffs.

Scary, isn't it? It is also scary to realize that the power of the articulate and brilliant analytic mind is not confined to Wall Street, but is pervasive throughout Western society. Our MBA and other professional schools continue to grind out technocrats. We have become so caught up in our scientific methodology that if something cannot be measured or counted, it will not be believed. As a result, we tend to adapt the world to our belief systems, rather than try to understand it as it is. In dealing with a changing world, we often try to "catch water in a bucket" rather than go with the flow.

As the story goes, God and the Devil were debating about the goodness of man as they walked down a seldom-used road. While they were arguing about man's inner nature, they noticed the lonely figure of a man approaching them. Suddenly, the man bent over and picked up a grain of "truth." "You see," God exclaimed, "man just discovered 'truth' and that proves that he is good." The Devil replied, "Ah, so he did. But you don't understand the nature of man. Soon he'll try to organize it, and then he'll be mine!"

My broker advised me to go heavily into stocks.
. . . What does your broker recommend?

2

THE TAO OF DOW

The masters of life know the Way. They listen to the voice within them, the voice of wisdom and simplicity, the voice that reasons beyond cleverness and knows beyond knowledge. That voice is not just the power and property of a few, but has been given to everyone.
—BENJAMIN HOFF,
  The Tao of Pooh

May the force be with you.
—OBI-WAN KENOBI,
  Star Wars

No one could accuse Lao Tsu, the founder of Taoism, of being a champion of logic. He felt that if mankind were to "discard knowledge, the people will be benefited a hundredfold." If he were alive today he would likely frown on Wall Street's analytic ants scurrying from company to company in search of EPSEI (earnings-per-share estimate information). Lao Tsu would not likely fall into the Devil's hands by overly organizing truth.

Though the philosophy of Taoism is marvelously simple, it is difficult to describe in words. The first line of Lao

Tsu's great book, the _Tao Te Ching_, reads, "The Tao that can be told is not the eternal Tao." The Tao means "the Way," the way of the universe that cannot be adequately described in words.

Taoism, along with Confucianism and Buddhism, is one of the three great philosophic teachings of China. Like the Judeo-Christian tradition, it has a concept of duality—but with an important difference. The Judeo-Christian tradition emphasizes _opposing_ dualities, such as heaven and hell, good and evil, God above and Devil below. Taoism, on the other hand, stresses unity and the interrelationship of all things. Its notion of duality is one of polarity, in which the yin (female) and the yang (male), good and evil, pleasure and pain, are seen as complementary poles that cannot exist without one another.

Despite these commonalities and the fact that Lao Tsu and Confucius were likely contemporaries some 2,500 years ago, Taoism and Confucianism are best known for their contrasts. Confucius believed in the worship of ancestors, strict morality, high court etiquette, and the importance of rules and names. Taoism, on the other hand, advocates cooperation with the universal laws of nature while avoiding the artificial doctrines invented by man. As Lao Tsu stated, "To attain knowledge, add things every day; to obtain wisdom, remove things every day." Knowledge is the goal of Confucius, whereas Taoism strives for wisdom. Confucius is remembered as one of the world's great scholars, whereas Lao Tsu, in saying that the "sage sees and hears no more than an infant sees and hears," can be seen as a keen but simple observer of nature.

Buddhism arrived in China some 1,500 years after the advent of the other two great teachings. Imported from India, Buddhism viewed life as a dusty, unpleasant existence that one endured until reaching Nirvana, the "land without wind," upon death. Despite its rather uncompromising attitude, Buddhism became mellowed over time by the basically optimistic nature of the Chinese people. After absorbing elements of both Taoism and Confucianism, Buddhism traveled to Japan and became the cornerstone of Zen, which, like Taoism, rejects verbal teachings and disregards logic.

Taoism, due in large part to its metamorphic and undefined character, has gone through many transformations over the ages, including many bizarre activities such as the practice of alchemy in the search for the elixir of eternal life. Chinese history relates the story of the emperor Hsien Tsung, who became intrigued with Liu Pi, a Taoist alchemist. Liu Pi persuaded the emperor that he had the elixir of immortality. So, in A.D. 820, the emperor ate the longevity pill and died forthwith.

Taoism also produced some bizarre sexual rituals. Holmes Welch, in his book *Taoism: The Parting of the Way*, refers to a kind of sexual version of "musical chairs," called the Union of Breath dance. Here the objective of the male partner is to be with as many female partners as possible without experiencing an orgasm. These practices resulted in such stories as those of the legendary Yellow Emperor who was said to have had intercourse with 1,200 concubines at one time.

The birthdate of Lao Tsu, which translates to mean "ancient thinker," is traditionally accepted to be around the year 600 B.C. Though this date is often debated, there is considerably more controversy over whether or not Lao Tsu in fact ever existed! The original manuscript of the *Tao Te Ching* has long since disappeared, adding further mystery to this mystical philosophy.

Taoism has survived and flourished over the years because of its inherent flexibility. As Lao Tsu said, "That which is the most yielding eventually overcomes what is most resistant." The *Tao Te Ching* offers something to everyone, depending on the needs of the reader. Everyone is free to interpret it in his own fashion.

An example of Taoism's durability occurred when Kublai Khan, the most famous descendant of the Mongol conqueror Genghis Khan, ordered the destruction of all Chinese works on religion, sorcery, and philosophy—with one exception: the *Tao Te Ching*, which he declared to be the greatest of all Chinese books.

Another factor in the success of the Taoist principles can be related to Lao Tsu's belief in anonymity. Since his teachings were not personalized or labeled, Lao Tsu's principles have had their greatest successes under other labels (such as Zen).

Today there is a growing Western interest in Taoism, influenced in part by Alan Watts, the renowned interpreter of Eastern ways, who believed that a widespread absorption of the profound wisdom of Taoism could transform the West. Marilyn Ferguson, in her new-age book *The Aquarian Conspiracy*, feels that the interest in Taoism relates to a strong societal interest in the unknown, the known having failed us so often. Conditions appear to be ripe for our Western culture to be cross-pollinized by this simple ancient philosophy.

Marshall McLuhan felt that our technological revolution helped popularize Eastern thought; "electric circuitry," he says, "is Orientalizing the West. The contained, the distinct, the separate—our Western legacy—are being replaced by the flowing, the unified, the fused." McLuhan's observation becomes more relevant as the rate of world change intensifies.

In a world where dynamic change is a constant, one has to go with the flow in order to survive. As Lao Tsu said, "To resist change is like holding your breath—if you persist, you will die." Therefore, Lao Tsu's advice that "man must accept motion, must live with motion, and must know himself to be forever moving" is even more relevant today than when first uttered. Unfortunately, Western mentality with its analytic ways tends to resist change by making fixity out of flux, or as Lao Tsu would say, it tries to understand running water by catching it in a bucket.

Since one cannot analyze change until after it has happened, our Western approach to information leaves us dealing with events after the fact rather than as a part of the flow. Moreover, our societal disease of what I call "analexia" (our conviction that if something cannot be analyzed or measured, it is not real) is accompanied by our passion for numbers.

By depending on expertise, we have become less dependent on ourselves. By so downgrading our trust in our intuitions and feelings, we settle too often for the false comforts of doctrines and beliefs. Considering the predictive records of economists and other information specialists, it is quite clear that such trust has too often been unrewarded. In effect, by attempting to fit life's events into the framework of rigid form, we tend to exhaust our energies by trying to freeze the flow of the current. For these reasons, Taoism has the potential of being a catalyst for freeing the "fixity" of the Western view.

But what, after all, is Taoism? What is it about this ancient philosophy that has influenced so many, including this author? What is it about Lao Tsu, a simple man of few words, that has caught the imaginations of generations of people around the world?

His philosophy is simple, but not easy. His main principles, for instance, fall under such improbable headings as Wu Wei (the law of reverse effort), the newborn child, catching running water in a bucket, P'u (the uncarved block), Te (being with the Tao), and Judo (the "gentle way" of martial arts).

The Tao means "the Way"—the underlying nature of the universe. It is as if there were a central axis around which everything revolves in an interrelated way. Though this concept could provide a rationale for astronomy, Lao Tsu was not interested in observing planetary activities, but rather those of nature and inner man. For Lao Tsu, "without going beyond one's nature, one can achieve ultimate wisdom."

To achieve wisdom and power, you merely need to understand the five simple workings of nature that reflect universal principles, then learn to cooperate with events rather than fight them. Though Lao Tsu believes in the interconnectedness of all things, he does not advocate predestination, but says rather that one who possesses Te (the power of being in tune with the Tao) can positively influence his life by observing and fitting into the natural flow of things. By understanding the nature of inner man, the Taoist can turn human forces to his own advantage. Successful living, like surfing, is the art of picking the right wave to ride.

In Taoism opposites are in harmony, not in rebellion,

with the fundamental laws of the universe, and it is therefore not appropriate to debate their differences. Yin and yang, long and short, life and death are fused into one, as each depends on its counterpart for full completion. In fact, each can be seen only in terms of its relevance to its counterpart. By not favoring one side or the other, the Taoist is able to appreciate the virtues of both. Man's artificial rules of good and evil, right and wrong, do not necessarily fit the Tao, "the way of the universe."

Another central principle of Taoism is called the uncarved block (P'u), which is the natural, unspoiled, simple, and honest quality of both man and nature. The uncarved block is man's original nature, free from hostility and aggression. The nearest human thing representing the uncarved block is the newborn child. "The sage sees and hears no more than an infant sees and hears," Lao Tsu states.

To utilize the power of the uncarved block, one has to return to childlike ways by unlearning the rules of man and society, and thus be free to allow the unconscious mind to work effectively. We should learn to appreciate the uncarved block, the inner virtue, in all things. Such awareness will result in our not trying to make something or someone be different from its true nature (e.g., by not putting square pegs into round holes). Thus, one should "accept what is weak for what strength it has, and use what is dim for the light it gives." The sage does not desire to change others.

Lao Tsu, perhaps in part as a rebuff to the many followers of Confucius, was an outright ridiculer of scholars, who, he felt, devised rules that conflicted with the basic laws of nature and thus interfered with our ability to be in touch with our unconscious, our uncarved block. Scholars' conscious minds, he felt, acquired knowledge for the sake of knowledge and erected word barriers between themselves and common people in order to appear superior. Lao Tsu felt that reality should not be theorized about (as in the West), but directly perceived through intuitive and experiential understanding.

Lao Tsu suggests using observation to understand the laws of nature and the universe. But what about understanding the laws of man, which he admits tend to be artificial? In dealing with one's fellowman, Lao Tsu suggests employing the principles of water.

- Of all substances "nothing is weaker than water; yet, for attacking what is hard and tough, nothing surpasses it."

- Water seeks the lowest place and thus is humble and receptive, like the female yin.

- Water adapts to the shape of the container in which it is placed and is therefore flexible.

- Like the universe itself, water is in constant motion.

In dealing with one's fellowman, Lao Tsu recommends that one be humble, flexible, adaptable, and accepting of change as a way of life. The principle Lao Tsu calls Wu Wei, which literally means "not doing," is the doctrine of inaction, sometimes called the law of reverse effort. Wu Wei does not mean total passivity, but rather the avoidance of forcing, of hostile or aggressive acts. Wu Wei means rolling with the punches, swimming with the current, and winning by attraction and attitude rather than by deed and compulsion. Examples of the law of reverse effort are many. For instance, when you try to float, you sink, but when you try to sink, you float. When you try to remember a name, you can't, but when you stop thinking about it, it appears forthwith. When you hold your breath, you lose it, but when you let it go, you regain it. Wu Wei means succeeding by attitude rather than action; it is having the power of the infectious wish that comes from certain virtues such as compassion, moderation, and humility.

In applying the principle of Wu Wei to the affairs of men, Lao Tsu made reference to government and teaching. In government, one should "govern a large country as you would cook a small fish—lightly." Lao Tsu would not recommend, as did Confucius, that copious rules be imposed upon people, for "the more laws are enacted and taxes assessed, the greater the number of law-breakers and tax evaders." The sage does not teach by telling others what to do; he leads by example. Education should be focused primarily on recapturing faculties that have been allowed to go astray in the stress of life.

When it comes to the stock market, Taoism can be used to justify many different methodologies. For instance, the technician would encourage one to "go with the flow" of what others are buying and selling. The fundamentalist would say that successful investing depends upon knowing the "way" of the economy, industries, and companies. Finally, the contrarian would advise generosity, like "the sage who prefers being the creditor," by giving others the stocks they want and buying those that they don't.

Perhaps this book will help you decide which Tao principles will work for you.

3
OUR TWO BRAINS

A scholar named Wang
Laughed at my poems
The accents are wrong
He said
Too many beats
The meter is poor
The wording impulsive.

I laughed at his poems
As he laughed at mine
They read like
The words of a blind man
Describing the sun.
—HAN-SHAN,
  Taoist poet

95 percent of what is known
about our brains, we have
learned in the last ten years.
—TONY BUZAN,
  The Brain User's Guide

The World's Smartest Man finds himself together with the president of the United States, a priest, and a hippie in a plane doomed to crash. On board are only three parachutes, which prompts the president to take one immediately and jump, with the declaration that he owes it to the American people to survive. The World's Smartest Man next steps forth, claims that his life is an irreplaceable asset to humanity, and exits. The priest looks at the hippie and says: "I have lived my life and now it is in God's hands; you take the last parachute." The hippie replies: "No sweat, Padre, we're both safe; the World's Smartest Man jumped out with my knapsack!"

Judging from the reactions I've received to this story, I'd say that people seem to find it entirely plausible that the "world's smartest man" could be so dumb. Such a paradox is not only curious, but may have many implications for stock market investors. Don't we all know people who are intellectually brilliant, but who lack common sense?

As a starting point in our examination of our impractical genius, several people were asked to list the characteristics of the "world's smartest man." Interestingly, their answers could be classified easily into positive and negative categories:

A walking computer	Impractical
Educated—Ph.D.	Has little common sense
An expert	Won't admit he's wrong
Knows about everything	Close-minded
High IQ—genius	Absentminded; careless
More knowledgeable than others	Unwilling to see others' point of view
Intellectual	Thinks he has all the answers
Knows a great many statistics	Sees the trees, not the forest

These responses suggest that there is a flip side or possible liabilities and flaws for those who are exceptionally "brilliant." Looking at the brain and how it operates, it is interesting to see that we have two brains within our neocortex: a left and right hemisphere. Furthermore, each person is dominated by either one side or the other. Though these twin hemispheres look alike, recent brain research indicates they control very different functions.

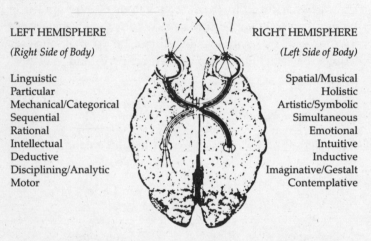

LEFT HEMISPHERE

(Right Side of Body)

Linguistic
Particular
Mechanical/Categorical
Sequential
Rational
Intellectual
Deductive
Disciplining/Analytic
Motor

RIGHT HEMISPHERE

(Left Side of Body)

Spatial/Musical
Holistic
Artistic/Symbolic
Simultaneous
Emotional
Intuitive
Inductive
Imaginative/Gestalt
Contemplative

As the diagram shows, our left hemisphere, which controls the right side of the body, is analytically oriented. It reasons logically and sequentially and is responsible for our speech. It is adept at math, accounting, languages, science, and writing. Like a computer, it is programmable and is nurtured by our highly analytic educational process. The properties of the left brain are not unique; man has developed computers that can duplicate those functions.

Our right-brain hemisphere, which controls the movements of the left side of the body, *is* unique. It operates nonsequentially, is intuitive, artistic, has feelings, is gestalt-oriented (sees the forest and not just the trees), and controls our visual perceptions. Since it is nonverbal, it communicates to us through dreams and "gut reactions." The right hemisphere provides and stores all of our nonverbal experience—a vast amount of input, certainly much more than we can verbally retrieve from our left brain.

The characteristics of the "world's smartest man" are those that correspond to the left hemisphere and can thus be measured by IQ testing (in cases where a diseased right hemisphere has been totally removed by surgery, patients often show little or no decline in IQ scores). His liabilities center around his lack of right-brained perceptions. Thus, our intellectually brilliant genius turns out not to be a person who possesses wisdom, but rather one who has imbalanced thought processes. He may be more knowledgeable than any other member of the human race, but at the same time be incapable of sensing the real world around him (let alone make a visual distinction between a parachute and a knapsack).

Our society would tend to categorize the "world's smartest man" as "the best and the brightest," despite his imbalanced brain, and elevate him to an important position of leadership. There his incompleteness, which he would be the last to admit, would result in disastrous decisions made by using only half a brain.

Though great strides have been made in understanding our brains, we still know precious little about how our minds actually work. Except for outer space, it is the area of our greatest scientific ignorance. It is also one of our areas of greatest discovery, for as Tony Buzan, author of *The Brain User's Guide*, states, we have learned 95 percent of what we know about our brains in the last ten years. And considering that there are over half a million papers per year published on the brain, it is likely that Buzan and others will still be able to make the "95 percent" claim ten years hence.

Our brain weighs approximately three pounds, or on the average about 2 percent of our body weight. It uses 20 percent of our oxygen supply and is similar to a vast and complicated electrical network, as it generates 40 volts of electricity (enough to dimly light a small bulb). It is composed of billions of brain cells that, in turn, are connected by billions of synapses. The human brain is so intricate, vast, and complex that a computer looks primitive in comparison. Estimates vary, but it would take several gymnasiums full of the most powerful microcomputers to duplicate the capabilities of just one brain. It is also estimated that we use but a small fraction of the potential of our brains (from 1 to 5 percent).

The amazing capabilities of the human mind can be seen in young children. Recent discoveries indicate that the ability of babies to perform such tasks as facial recognition is much greater than previously believed. Young children also have twice as many synaptic connections as the mature adult. As a result, until the age of six a child will learn vocabulary at the astonishing average rate of one word every two waking hours and can easily learn a second foreign language without any trace of accent. At birth our brains are approximately 25 percent of their adult size, but within only two years they reach 75 percent or more of their size at full maturity!

Seven hundred years ago, Roger Bacon commented that "there are two modes of knowing, those of argument and experience." The Hopi Indians have for centuries referred to one hand for writing and one for music. These examples—the poet's ageless dilemma of the heart versus the brain—all point to man's intuitive sense of his underlying duality. Now, thanks to the work of Dr. Roger W. Sperry, Nobel prize winner for medicine, Dr. Joseph Bogen, and others, man's duality has been linked to the physiological makeup of the brain.

In 1953 Dr. Sperry began experimenting with cats at Cal Tech. By severing the corpus callosum (a bundle of nerve fibers that connect the two hemispheres), he discovered that while one side of the brain could be trained, the other side would remain ignorant. Sperry was thus able to infer that each half of the brain was capable of functioning independently. In 1961 Sperry broadened his research efforts by working with patients who had split-brain operations in order to remedy severe cases of epilepsy. Epileptic seizures are caused by electronic waves moving back and forth between the two hemispheres. By severing the corpus callosum, not only was the epilepsy stopped, but patients seemed surprisingly normal after the operation.

Soon after the operation on one patient, referred to as "W.J.," Dr. Sperry and his assistants, Levy and Gazzaniga, discovered some very odd things. W.J. could carry out verbal commands such as "raise your hand" or "bend your leg"—but only with the right side of his body. His left side could not respond, since its nonverbal command center (the right brain) could not understand language. When blindfolded, W.J. was unable to tell which part of his body was being touched. Other oddities surfaced, such as instances when he would pull down his pants with one hand while pulling them up with the other. Once, when he grabbed a knife with his left hand and threatened his wife, his right hand came to her rescue by grabbing the other hand. His left, logical mind prevailed over his right!

Though one side of the body is controlled by the opposite side of the brain, our eyes, which are the only area outside our skulls that contain brain cells, transmit stimuli to both brains through split fields of vision. The left field of both eyes reports to the right brain, whereas the right field records its images in the left hemisphere. Thus, to read facial expressions one can achieve heightened awareness by looking slightly to the right of the face so that the image will be recorded primarily in the left visual field and thus transmitted to the emotional, intuitive right brain. In like manner, fighter pilots in World War II were trained to aim slightly to the right of their targets during dogfights.

To further test split-brained patients, experiments have been conducted where pictures were flashed to their separate visual fields. For example, if the word "pencil" was flashed in the left visual field, the patient, even though he could not verbalize the object, could easily pick out the pencil with his left hand from a group of objects. When asked why he picked out the object, the patient would typically say, "Well, I must have done it subconsciously." This tendency of the left brain to rationalize and take credit for actions controlled by the right brain is common, a point Thomas R. Blakeslee makes in his book *Right Brain*. As this tendency appears so quickly among split-brained patients after surgery, Blakeslee infers that our normal brain has the same tendency, that it is already an ingrained habit in all of us.

Other insights about the functions of the bicameral hemispheres have come from the study of patients with brain damage. Since each hemisphere has its separate circulatory system, strokes commonly affect only one half of the brain (and thus the opposite side of the body). Where there is damage to the right, nonverbal side, the patient can still talk and understand the literal meaning of words perfectly, but will not be able to deal with emotional tone, inflections, and metaphors. The patient can speak, but no longer remembers melodies. An interesting example of the opposite situation—a stroke damaging the left, verbal hemisphere—occurred in an individual who was a composer. After the stroke, he became speechless, but went on to compose his best music. He couldn't write notes, but he could play, hear, and remember them, thus showing the musical talent of his right hemisphere.

More information has been provided by the work of Robert Ornstein and others in measuring electrical activities of the hemispheres in order to determine what part of the brain was active during various mental tasks. This research indicates that when one hemisphere is active, the other is often idle (will emit alpha waves). Thus, when most individuals are balancing their checkbooks, their left hemisphere will be active while their right brain will emit alpha waves (be resting). Conversely, while listening to music, the right hemisphere will be active and the left in alpha state (except with professional musicians, where the reverse will be true).

DOMINANCE

It is becoming increasingly clear that it is important for each hemisphere to do the mental task for which it is best suited—to match the right tool with the right job. This is easier said than done, as our minds are often dominated by one side or the other, and we have a strong tendency to rely too heavily on our dominant mode.

Each of us shows a dominant preference for one side of our body or the other; cases of true ambidexterity are rare. We have a dominant hand, foot, and even eye. (Note: To test for your dominant eye, point to a small object across the room and shut first one eye and then the other. The eye that is "on target" is your dominant eye.) There is a good reason for dominance; if one side did not control the other, we would often end up like Buridan's Ass (the symbol of indecisiveness because it starved to death equidistant between two bales of hay). There is, in fact, growing evidence that dyslexia occurs in cases where there are verbal skills in both hemispheres. Indecisive mental processing occurs as the two sides vie for control.

An illustration of the different modes of brain dominance can be seen in how two individuals might build a model airplane. The left-brain oriented person, comfortable with linear, step-by-step processes, would tend to carefully follow the directions from A to B to C, etc., until completed. A right-brainer might well throw away the directions, place all the parts in front of him, look at the picture of the finished product, and then begin assemblage. This same "right-brained" type would probably do well with geometry because of its preference for spatial relationships, whereas algebra's symbolic, sequential orientation would prove more difficult. A left-brainer, as you might suspect, would tend to prefer algebra over geometry. When traveling, the left-brainer would prefer to have linear directions, whereas his counterpart would much prefer a map. More and more companies are recognizing these different preferences and are issuing instructions in both modes, visual and verbal.

It is not uncommon to find an A student who can name all the parts of the automobile and give an impressive dissertation on the principles of the internal combustion engine. However, when it comes to actually repairing a car, such an individual often becomes completely lost and can be run in circles by the high-school dropout who cannot explain the principles of anything, but can easily take the car apart and put it back together again.

In observing business executives on the job, Dr. Henry Mintzberg from McGill University noted that businessmen tend to gravitate toward their mental dominance; the analytic left-brained types usually end up in staff positions, whereas high-level managers tend to be right-brained intuitive types. This generality does not always hold true. Psychiatrists' couches contain many mismatches. As Mintzberg stated in his award-winning *Harvard Business Review* article (May 1975), "Planning on the Left Side and Managing on the Right," "The policymaker conceives the strategy in holistic [right-brained] terms and the rest of the hierarchy implements it in sequence." Mintzberg adds that the typical top manager "works at an unrelenting pace, that his activities are characterized by brevity, variety, and discontinuity." Mintzberg takes issue with the business school concept that executives are scientific practitioners; in reality, they are often guided by nonlinear, gestalt processes.

While at General Electric, Ned Herrmann developed a test for determining an individual's brain dominance. Continuing his work with Applied Creative Services in Lake Lure, North Carolina, Herrmann has tested over 7,000 people and finds that dominance is not a simple either/or situation. His studies indicate that most individuals have multiple dominances, say, with a major left dominance, but with a right subdominance. He concludes that there are actually four basic modes of dominance, as described in greater detail in Chapter 11.

Herrmann's studies also tend to confirm Mintzberg's conclusion that in business individuals tend to seek occupations that fit their dominant mode. He developed the following chart from cross-reference analysis of the 7,000 individuals he has tested:

THE HERRMANN OCCUPATIONAL PROFILE

LEFT-BRAIN ORIENTED	RIGHT-BRAIN ORIENTED
Planners	Policymakers
Lawyers	Artists
Editors	Poets
Technologists	Sculptors
Writers	Politicians
Bookkeepers	Playwrights
Critics	Musicians
Management scientists	Philosophers
Administrators	Architects
Doctors	Clowns
Authors	Cartoonists
Tax experts	Entrepreneurs
Researchers	Dancers
Publishers	Top Executives

As interesting as the above delineation may be, Herrmann would be the first to point out that we are talking about *dominance*, not either/or thinking. Those who are most successful in their careers are integrating qualities of both halves of their brains in their thought processes. It is also important to note that the chart does not happen to mention that Wall Street research analysts are strongly left-brain oriented, whereas portfolio managers tend to be more oriented to the right hemisphere.

Drawing by Lorenz; © 1977 The New Yorker Magazine, Inc.

"Foster here is the left side of my brain, and Mr. Hoagland is the right side of my brain."

4

THE BICAMERAL PERSPECTIVE

When opposites supplement each other, everything is harmonious.
—LAO TSU

We are at war between consciousness and nature, between the desire for permanence and the fact of flux. It is ourself against ourselves.
—ALAN WATTS,
The Wisdom of
Insecurity

Research discoveries about the bicameral mind have many implications, not least of which is that our Western society is an imbalanced one. The industrial revolution, followed by a scientific one, has resulted in our paying homage to left-hemispheric skills, such as those of the "world's smartest man," at the expense of right-brained sensing. Our culture has elevated verbal and written expression, mathematical aptitude, and logical analysis, while downgrading emotional, intuitive, and artistic thought processes.

The Renaissance is the last time there was a whole-brained societal balance in the West, for during that period there was a balance between science and the arts. As the industrial revolution gained steam, left-hemispheric logic became an increasingly valued commodity. Industrialization created many uncreative clerical jobs, as well as production lines that required repetitive, sequential tasks. With the advent of the computer, which "thinks" sequentially in digital form, the left brain was given a powerful tool to extend its capabilities.

Our modern obsession with numbers has resulted in a "Cognitive Era," and our obsession with measurement has created a prevalent philosophy that if it can't be counted, it doesn't count. Though we are told not to compare apples and oranges, we continually do so by translating them into numbers. In the process, we tend to lose track of their intangible properties such as taste, nutrition, and aesthetics.

An increase in specialization has accompanied the rise of science and technology. Specialized left-brain oriented professions have proliferated, and aided by the perception that the government saved America from the Great Depression, the "FDR syndrome" has developed. This refers to our society's awe of experts, the idea that someone else—the government, doctor, lawyer, educator, etc.—is better able to look after our lives than we are. This syndrome has resulted in a lack of confidence in ourselves.

Our passion for measurement has made our destinies more and more determined by IQ and other tests that measure only half our brains. Those who qualify for college and graduate schools by SAT and other test scores are not necessarily those who are balanced and who have good judgment, but rather those with imbalanced, left-brained mental specialization. In turn, these scholars swell the ranks of the educators and thus perpetuate the system.

Has this shift to our "scientific" logical mind worked? In one sense, its track record has certainly been impressive. After years of slow evolution, man's ability to pass his knowledge on in written form to the next generation has resulted in advancements that have allowed us to put a man on the moon, split the atom, and communicate through the airways. The fact that 90 percent of the scientists who have ever lived are alive today is a rather impressive statement about the growth dynamics of the Cognitive Era.

THE RISE OF RIGHT-HEADEDNESS

The comic strip character Pogo and his pals on a snowy day walked around a large tree and spotted their own footprints. After declaring that he had found the enemy, Pogo began following the tracks. When he finally realized the obvious, he stated, "We have found the enemy and they is us!"

Just a decade ago American business managers were considered to be the best in the world. With a societal richness of economists (ten out of the last seventeen Nobel prize–winning economists have been Americans), computer scientists, MBAs, and other experts, it seemed that we could not help but maintain our "number-one" ranking. But it was not to be, as our management has become a source of national embarrassment.

It is becoming increasingly clear that our trend toward technocratic, left-brained specialization in business has reached a point of diminishing returns. These very experts in whom business has placed its trust have failed by not being sensitive to changing situations. Furthermore, they have created an overload of information that has often obscured reality. Like Till Eulenspiegel, the sorcerer's apprentice of German folklore who became a victim of his own magic, we have become victims of our own methodology. We have relied too heavily on our left brains, thus denying the intuitive visionary qualities of our right hemispheres that so well served our forefathers.

The best-selling 1983 book *In Search of Excellence*, by Thomas J. Peters and Robert H. Waterman, Jr., looks at America's best-run companies in order to see why they have been successful. Their conclusions are clear: The best-run companies do not depend on rational models of management controls; rather, they excel by creating a positive environment for their managers and employees to trust and use their right brains.

A similar awareness is developing about the infallibility of our professions. A recent poll ranked lawyers as being perceived as only slightly more trustworthy than used-car salesmen. The trend toward holistic medicine, and the brisk sales of the Merck Manual and other diagnostic books to the home market, indicate a growing distrust of doctors. Such increasing distrust of our experts, combined with growing political conservatism that is pressuring for less government, suggests that the FDR syndrome is subsiding. Perhaps we are learning to trust ourselves again.

As we gain more self-confidence, we are coming to rely more on our own ability to sense reality directly, and, conversely, we are less likely to blindly follow the experts who claim to have all the answers. Since direct sensing is best performed by the right hemisphere, such a trend implies a shift away from our imbalanced cognitive values and toward more whole-brained thinking. The Cognitive Era appears to be in its twilight.

One hypothesis for the decline in SAT scores for college candidates is that the scores reflect not a decline in our youths' collective wisdom, but a shift to an increased reliance on their right hemispheres. Today's students, having been brought up by television (the average child today spends more time watching TV than in the classroom) and then video games, have developed increased visual and spatial abilities. Since vision is the most information rich of all our senses, the decline in SAT scores may simply reflect a decline in measurable cognitive functions, while visual skills (immeasurable by current standardized tests) may be increasing.

TAOISM AND THE HEMISPHERES

By declaring in the first line of the *Tao Te Ching* that the "way of the universe" cannot be adequately described in words, Lao Tsu shows his disdain for the language skills that are identified with the left hemisphere. He later adds, "Those who know do not speak; those who speak do not know," thus leaving us with little doubt about how he would view the "articulate incompetent." For Lao Tsu, man needs to overcome a lifetime habit of expressing thoughts only in words.

Lao Tsu recommended that we "discard knowledge and the people would benefit a hundredfold." Of man, he said, "Even though he may be a 'walking encyclopedia,' he is really a misguided fool." He also said, "If we stop fussing about grammatical trivialities, we will get along much better." Such statements indicate that Lao Tsu not only placed little value on the scholarship qualities of the left hemisphere, but also viewed them as frankly negative traits. "Day after day the overzealous student stores up facts for future use. But he will discard formula after formula, until he reaches the conclusion, Let nature take its course." In short, Lao Tsu feels that "expertise" does not work, that left-hemispheric logic is incapable of leading us to the higher wisdom of intuitive knowing. He complains about the scholars who study for the sake of knowledge and who then create a barrier of words between themselves and common people. As Lao Tsu laments, "Nature's way is simple and easy, but men prefer the intricate and the artificial." Therefore, "The wise are not learned and the learned are not wise."

"The power of intuitive understanding will protect you from harm until the end of your days." "The sage is guided by what he feels." Such statements by Lao Tsu show his preference for those qualities of the right hemisphere. True education comes from unlearning the artificial rules of man, as indicated by the saying, "The sage sees and hears no more than an infant sees and hears." Teaching should not be done by describing and pointing out differences, but by example. Understanding is a matter of intuitive sensing, not the result of some discipline. By stating, "Without going beyond one's nature, one can achieve ultimate wisdom," Lao Tsu is giving right-brained knowing the highest accolade.

Throughout the *Tao Te Ching*, Lao Tsu downgrades the role of logical, verbal, sequential thinking at all turns, whether it relates to areas of human interaction, affairs of state, or the discovery of wisdom. He believes that "the way of the universe" can be understood only through perception of nature, by using the attributes of the right brain. Since man and nature are in constant motion, a notion Fritjor Capra in his book *The Tao of Physics* claims is being verified by recent scientific findings, Lao Tsu feels that the world needs to be sensed directly. By saying that running water can't be understood by catching it in a bucket, he is observing the inability of the left hemisphere to deal with motion and change.

Lao Tsu's constant bias for right-brained qualities is so strong and consistent that his writing can be viewed as an appeal for right-headedness. One could even go so far as to call the right brain the "Lao Tsu brain." The increasing popularity of Taoism in the West is another confirmation that the Cognitive Era is gradually giving way to a greater increase in right-brained values. However, our society is still dominated by left-hemispheric values, and if Lao Tsu were to reappear today, the "experts" would no doubt echo the sentiments Confucius expressed after the only meeting of the two philosophers: "I just don't understand Lao Tsu." In effect, what they would be saying is that they just do not understand the nonverbal, intuitive, feeling side of their own cerebrum.

RIGHT-HEADED DISCRIMINATION

A recent study indicates that left-handers have a 250 percent greater incidence of ulcers than right-handers. This rather startling bit of information suggests what most left-handers have known for years, that society discriminates against them. Since the left hand is controlled by the right brain, such discrimination is really also a bias against our intuitive right minds!*

Evidence of such discrimination is easy to find; all one needs to do is reach for a dictionary. *Webster's Third International Dictionary* describes left-handed as:

a. marked by clumsiness or ineptitude; awkward
b. exhibiting deviousness or indirection; oblique, unintended
c. obs: given to malevolent scheming or contriving; sinister, underhand

These definitions become doubly interesting when one considers that they are the product of someone's left brain (an indication that our look-alike hemispheres tend to compete). Left is *gauche* in French and *sinistra* in Italian, and in Spanish the idiom for "to be clever" is *no ser zurdo*, which literally translates to mean "not to be left-handed."

In many societies the left hand is avoided for the rather practical reason that it is the hand used for personal hygiene after defecation. The English overlooked this fact many years ago when, to curry favor, they presented a Rolls-Royce to the king of Saudi Arabia. The king was less than thrilled and promptly gave the luxurious automobile to one of his brothers. Why? Because the king preferred to ride in the front seat and would rather be caught dead than sit at the left hand of the driver! His brother, on the other hand, preferred to ride in the backseat!

For years there has been what amounted to an active campaign to stamp out left-handedness. The Catholic

---

*Left-handedness is not a totally reliable test for intuitive dominance, as 15 percent of left-handers have their verbal skills located in their right hemisphere and another 15 percent have speaking ability in both hemispheres.

Church, for example, until this century would not admit lefties to the priesthood. Until recently, when babies showed left-handed preference, they were often switched to the right hand by switching the rattle, etc. Because this practice has virtually died out, the percentage of left-handers in our society has risen from 2 percent of our population in 1932 to the 10 percent level. (Stutterers have declined proportionally, as studies have shown that half of all stutterers were left-handers who were forced to switch.)

Though definitive studies have not yet been published about the brain dominance of minorities, there is an interesting possibility that blacks, Indians, and other minorities have been discriminated against not so much because of their skin color but because of their right-brained thought preference. One indication of their dominance is the success of blacks in basketball, a spatial, nonprogrammed sport if there ever was one. Seventy-two percent of the players in the NBA are black.

All of this is, of course, changing. Increasingly, minorities are scoring well on IQ tests and are being granted advanced degrees. In turn, they are assuming their places as doctors, lawyers, and in other professions. As their educational opportunities increase, it is becoming clear that they can develop analytic skills as well as anyone. Male

MOMMA by Mell Lazarus; Courtesy of Mell Lazarus and Field Newspaper Syndicate

teenage blacks, though considered by many to be the least employable group in our society, are actively winning money playing "shill games" on street corners. One wonders about the IQ levels of those who get taken. By the same token, as our society becomes more aware of the limitations of analytic thinking, it will also place an increased value on right hemispheric intuitive sensing.

BOOZE AS A BALANCER

The growth of left-brained thinking during the Cognitive Era has not been without its side effects. As we became more conditioned to distrust our own personal instincts in favor of "experts," we were also attracted to drinking to relieve our anxieties. Our left brain, the censor of our emotional right side, becomes tranquilized by alcohol. Just as meditation stills the left brain by giving it the simple task of repeating a mantra, so alcohol numbs the analytic mind so that our right hemisphere can be "let out of its cage." As we get high, physiologically speaking we are achieving a better balance and we thus tend to feel more complete. If this theory is correct, it may help explain why American Indians have trouble drinking. Since their left brain is their minority mode, drinking can more easily anesthetize their "censor," leaving them out of control.

John Marshall, founder of Right On, a Los Angeles organization that works with alcoholics ("experienced drinkers," as he prefers to call them), is fascinated with recent medical discoveries about the two brains. As he says, "Drinking is the easiest, most effective, most economical, and most accepted way to give the overworked half of the brain relaxation while the other half has a chance to express itself."

The Persians long ago sensed the relationship between booze and our two modes of thinking:

> "If an important decision is to be made [the Persians] discuss the question when they are drunk, and the following day the master of the house where the discussion was held submits their decision for reconsideration when they are sober. If they still approve it, it is adopted; if not, it is abandoned. Conversely, any decision they make when sober is reconsidered afterwards when they are drunk."—Herodotus, *The Histories* (ca. 450 B.C.), *Psychology Today,* December 1979.

THE JAPANESE

By relying too heavily on left-brained methodology, U.S. business managers have lost their market share in many key industries such as autos, steel, and electronics. In most cases, it has been the Japanese who have picked up the slack. Why have they succeeded? What qualities in their decision-making have made them so often right? Are they left- or right-brain dominated?

Though there do not appear to be any studies on Japanese brain dominance, the following quote certainly indicates "whole-brainedness." Mr. Shigem Okada, head of Mitsukoshi, Japan's largest department store, stated, "We succeed because we combine the pragmatic management techniques of the West with the spiritual, intuitive aspects of the East."

In the West one has to go back to the Renaissance to find such brain balance. The Japanese business success might be called a "business renaissance," brought about when their adoption of Western techniques reached a point equal to their traditional intuitive orientation. How long can this balance continue? It is hard to say, but considering the momentum of growth of their practical, left-brained side combined with the competitive and aggressive nature of their college students, one can foresee them becoming victims of their own methodology. It is ironic that this could occur at a time when the U.S. could experience an opposite trend toward more right-hemispheric or whole-brained decision-making.

WHERE WALL STREET IS HEADED

The dominant role of security analysts in the decision-making of professional investors is a key to Wall Street's mind-set; after all, they are called analysts. These highly paid researchers use logic by combing through the numbers, interviewing corporate managers, and then passing on their recommendations to the investment community as to whether a stock is a buy, hold, or sell.

As logical, brilliant, and hard-working as these professionals may be, the lack of success of their recommendations speaks for the ineffectiveness of their approach. Unlike the Japanese, analysts do not take a whole-brained approach to understanding the world. By applying left-brained logic to the illogical stock market, they often are using the wrong tool for the task. Though tests have not been done, it is quite likely that the majority of those investors who consistently outperform the market value their right-brained qualities, for that is the side that can best sense the rapidly changing world of the stock market. Lao Tsu, if he were a professional money manager, would probably not read institutional research reports, as he would feel that they would fill up the mind, preventing it from seeing the true nature of things.

5

BUTTERFLIES TO COCOONS

The sage is like a little child...so return to the beginning, become a child again.
—LAO TSU

It takes a long time to grow young.
—PABLO PICASSO

Our educational system and modern society generally discriminate against one whole half of the brain. In our present educational system, the attention given to the right hemisphere of the brain is minimal compared with the training lavished on the left side.
—DR. ROGER SPERRY

Just as a good football coach constantly stresses basics, it is important to discover what society's fundamentals are. To do this, we should look at our educational system. After all, its graduates are the ones who manage the companies listed on the New York Stock Exchange and who become Wall Street analysts.

A couple recently took their five-year-old son to interview for placement in the first grade of one of New York's most prestigious private boys' schools. As David's behavior was exemplary throughout the interview, his parents began to relax. Then the director of admissions, a stuffy young man with an English accent, asked David how many letters there were in his own name. "Four," declared David crisply. "I'm sorry, David, you are wrong," replied the interviewer, "there are five letters in your name." "No, four," stated David emphatically. "David," replied the interviewer, moving forward in his chair, "there are five letters in David." "Noooo, there are only four letters," David stated with set jaw. Eyes narrowing, the admissions director stated, "Five, D–A–V–I–D; that is five." "I knew you were wrong," David triumphed. "There are four, as everyone knows that there are two D's in David!"

For a scholar not to know something is practically a crime. Haven't we all had abuse heaped on us when we didn't get the answer that the teacher thought was right? The process is so intimidating that many adults have recurring nightmares about not having done their homework or about being unable to answer even one of the questions on a test. Consequently, most of us give a silent cheer when we hear the story about young David slaying the giant admissions director (who, incidentally, got the last word by not accepting David). Unfortunately, not many of us triumph over our educational system. It is so pervasive that sooner or later the inevitable happens. We start out as butterflies, and end up in cocoons.

Our typical educational format consists of a teacher imparting knowledge to a class, typically of fifteen to thirty students who are supposed to receive and absorb the intended messages. This educational system emphasizes being "right" at the expense of being open, and teaches our young to be still, to look to authority, and to construct certainties. It ingrains self-limiting behavior and promotes competition for the highest grades. As Marilyn Ferguson states in *The Aquarian Conspiracy,* "Conventional schools tend to be instruments of our greatest denial by breaking knowledge and experience into subjects, relentlessly turning wholes into parts, flowers into petals, history into events, without ever restoring continuity." She points out that what students need to learn is freedom, high expectations, awareness, patterns, connections, and creativity. She adds, "Whereas the young need some sort of initiation into an uncertain world, we give them bones from the culture's graveyards. Where they want the real thing, we give them abstract busy work, where they need to find meaning, the schools ask memorization, and discipline becomes divorced from intuition, patterns from parts."

Since we and many of our parents and grandparents went through a similar educational system, the process of educating our children is rarely questioned. So when we hear about the decline in SAT scores, we clamor for more of the "three R's." We remain silent when art is the first subject dropped from the curriculum when budgets are slashed. The result? More pressure, more inflexibility.

In Germany, grammar-school grades determine the course of future education. The decision is made in the fourth grade, when the child is about ten years old. Children who have earned on the average a B or higher go directly to the highest level of their three-branch system to prepare for university education. The others? They have little hope of even finishing high school and are likely to end up in apprenticeships or fall into the great mass of unskilled labor, where unemployment is high.

What are the effects on students where one's future is decided in the fourth grade? The all-important grammar-school averages are graded on the curve, beginning in second grade, "turning pigtailed classmates into arch-enemies," says Wilhelm Erbert, a Bavarian teacher and president of the World Teachers Association. "Instead of solidarity and community spirit," he says, "this system teaches competitive, elbowing techniques. Only the grades count. At the center is naked fear." As a result, one out of every five nine-year-olds is under psychiatric treatment, and one out of every three youngsters under sixteen suffers school anxiety—chronic stomach problems and/or headaches. It is not uncommon for nine-year-olds to have ulcers. Furthermore, an estimated 14,000 school-age children per year will attempt suicide, with more than 500 likely to succeed.

The German system appears to give the large bureaucracy that controls it just what it wants: ambitious, hard-working people who have learned that the best way to succeed is always to agree.

Will success in our educational system result in happiness and accomplishment so that the ends will justify the stressful means? Perhaps, but consider the results of an opinion poll on happiness that was published in the *Reader's Digest* in 1979. In that study, lawyers and doctors, the cream of the academic crop, ranked themselves as being *less* happy than most people. The doctors' opinions seem to be borne out by the interesting statistic that their life expectancy is five years less than the average.

And how have those with the highest grades and test scores, the ultimate product of our educational system, fared in the real world? Lewis B. Terman, a Stanford University professor, had interesting results from his now-famous study of high-IQ children, which he began in 1921. A group

of 1,528 young children with IQs above 135 were studied to
see how they would fare as adults. This six-decade study indicated that high IQs do not guarantee extraordinary accomplishment, since no one in the study achieved the sum-
mit of true genius. Though there were a few millionaires in
the group, none was awarded a Nobel prize or similar
honor, and there were hardly any distinguished artists.

Dr. Douglas H. Heath of Haverford College conducted a
study that also adds insight to this question. He did detailed
and exhaustive profiles of eighty-six male students at
Haverford, complete with personal interviews, test scores,
grades, college activities, and professor evaluations. Ten
years later Dr. Heath updated this profile. He was able to
locate sixty-seven of the original students and redid their
profiles—this time by interviewing them, their wives, their
coworkers and bosses as well as doing other appropriate
checks.

Incredible as it may seem, Dr. Heath discovered that the
students with a combination of high marks and high test
scores were actually having more difficulty adjusting to the
real world than the other students! Their marriages were
strained, their frustrations high, and their job results far
below their expectations. They tended to "analyze" rather
than "sense," and they competed rather than exercised
teamwork.

At Harvard Business School one study indicates that
Baker Scholars, the top 5 percent of the graduating class,
have earned an average salary that is less than the norm for
the class! As more evidence comes in, the case for "the best
and the brightest" dims.

EDUCATION AND THE SPLIT BRAIN

Mark Haroldsen, in his million-copy seller *How to Wake Up the Financial Genius Inside You,* lists eight qualities for success: belief, drive, desire, positive mental attitude, determination, discipline, excitement, and motivation. Despite the fact that of these eight qualities only one (discipline) is left-brain oriented, our Western educational system stresses verbal skills, sequential reasoning (cause and effect), scientific theory and, of course, reading, writing, and arithmetic. So constituted, there is a high correlation between high grades and IQ scores. Conversely, a study of engineering students by Don Taylor at Yale University indicates that there is virtually no correlation between grades and intuition. Considering such evidence, it is no wonder that Dr. Roger Sperry states, "Our educational system and modern society generally discriminate against one whole half of the brain. In our present educational system, the attention given to the right hemisphere of the brain is minimal compared with the training lavished on the left side." Such an educational bias, which is further reinforced by testing, has led to what I call "analexia," our society's compulsion to accept only what can be measured.

THE WHOLE-BRAINED APPROACH

If our educational system is left brained, and Lao Tsu, on the other hand, is right brained, whom should we believe? The answer is neither and both. Neither should be blindly followed, as to do so would be to act in a half-brained way. Nor should we ignore either, for each effectively represents its half of the brain. By understanding both and being able to use the correct hemisphere for the correct task, we can be more whole brained and effective in our decision-making.

Whole-brainedness, in turn, results in creative thought processes. In 1945 Graham Wallas developed in *The Art of Thought* a simple model for creativity that illustrates how creativity involves the whole brain. This model, which is the one most commonly used regarding creativity, consists of four stages: preparation, incubation, illumination, and verification.

Preparation is "doing your homework," researching the situation, searching for information, and it is best performed primarily by left-hemispheric skills. Incubation is "sleeping on it," taking a walk, or just reflecting. It takes place when the left brain idles (emits alpha waves) and the right mulls things over in its own nonverbal way. Illumination takes place when the two brains come together, when the left side is able to verbalize the intuitive understanding of the right. This coming together of the two minds can be so powerful that it often produces the enlightenment, the oceanic feeling, that sent Archimedes jumping out of the tub shouting "Eureka." Verification is the process whereby the left brain confirms the validity of the discovery.

Looking at Wallas's model for creativity, the stages of preparation, incubation, illumination, and verification can be classified hemispherically as left, right, both, and left. This suggests, indeed, that creativity and its counterpart, discovery, are whole brained. Einstein, when he quipped that he seemed to get his ideas while shaving in the morning, was in reality referring to the process whereby his left verbal hemisphere was combining with the right hemisphere's incubation that had been performed while he was asleep.

WHOLE-BRAINED EDUCATION

Lao Tsu's statement, "The wise are not learned and the learned are not wise," certainly does not suggest whole-brainedness, but rather the opposite: an either/or situation. It is here that hemispheric brain research would take issue with our venerable philosopher; it suggests that both hemispheres need development and interaction. Ideally, education should be designed to bolster both brains, as we need to learn to make our intuition an equal partner with logic. Considering the strong bias in favor of the left, how can the right also be educated?

Our educational system, of course, is not a total failure. It is doing an adequate job training the brain hemisphere that it is concerned about (even here there is mounting criticism of the system). Its major failing is that it misses the mark through omission; it does too little for the right. What is needed is not an elimination of what is being done, as Lao Tsu might advocate, but rather a scaling back of what is being taught and an increase in courses and methods that are not presently offered.

It is interesting that the development of most children's drawing skills tends to stop at about the same time, at the age of ten. Such a phenomenon is odd, when one considers that a child's hand-eye coordination continues to improve into his or her late teens. The problem is not with the hand, but the eye. As one's left brain fills up with knowledge, one's seeing ability decreases. As the brain is forced to economize on its inputs, it categorizes chairs, faces, etc. Such a phenomenon suggests that the incorporation of art in the school curriculum could give the right brain important training. Artistic development should greatly increase one's ability to see reality, motion, and change. In turn, the student would be better able to cope with change, as he would have less need to make fixity out of flux.

Several schools, such as the Magnet Art School in Eugene, Oregon, are extensively using art in the curriculum to develop young students. One school, the Mead School for Human Development in Greenwich, Connecticut, is achieving impressive results by incorporating the arts into a bicameral program.

The Mead School, which has been in existence for twelve years and goes through the eighth grade, spends only half as much time on the three R's as do most schools. By using the time so gained for arts (visual, musical, physical, as well as human theatrical arts), they are attempting to fortify both brains. Their use of the arts is not intended to develop professional artists or musicians, but rather to aid students in learning freedom, high expectations, pattern recognition, connections, and creativity—all right-brained attributes. Dr. Elaine de Beauport, the school's founder, feels that the nurturing of right-hemispheric skills increases the students' ability to perceive reality and sense creative solutions. In turn, they are able to have more confidence in their inner self and are thus less influenced by their peers (and other experts). They are better able to deal with the uncertain world and more likely to realize their potential.

Sounds good, but how have the results been? When Mead graduates enter a new school, they typically founder for one or two months while they figure out the ropes of the new system (i.e., imposed authority and rigid testing). After a period, though, good things begin to happen.

The Connecticut Association of Independent Schools' accreditation team did an official evaluation of the Mead School. What impressed them was the extent to which the graduates successfully learned in other private and public schools. Mead graduates go on to learn because they want to learn, not because they are forced. In addition, they appear able to survive in an intimidating system without being intimidated. Apparently, their training in the arts has helped develop a self-reliance that frees them from both peer and adult pressures.

At the Magnet Art School in Eugene, Oregon, students also spend less than half as much time on the three R's as do their counterparts in Eugene's traditional schools. According to a 1977 *Saturday Review* article, "Why Children Should Draw," compared with twenty-nine other schools in their district, Magnet Art's sixth grade tied for first place in reading and for fifth place in math.

This is not to suggest that the Mead School and Magnet Art School have reached educational perfection. We still know little about how the right brain works, let alone how to educate it. Moreover, the parents of children enrolled in these schools have mixed feelings about the programs. Nonetheless, these pioneer schools merit monitoring, as they may well be more similar to a typical school in the year 2000 than are today's "average" schools.

HIGHER EDUCATION AND LOWER SATISFACTION

Ignorance of the development of the right hemisphere in the lower grades is a sin of missed opportunities.

However, by the time the bias of our educational system has reached the graduate level, most students suffer from an almost permanent form of brain damage, "analexia." This ailment is a condition in which the student is able to recognize only what can be counted and analyzed. In most cases this condition has the side effect of an atrophied right brain.

Concerned about why fellow graduates of Harvard Medical School were so often disappointments as practicing doctors, Carlton Akins and Peter Ahrens conducted a study of the medical school to determine how it could be improved. Their conclusions, presented in a report to their Alumni Council, contained a great deal of criticism.

The Akins/Ahrens report pointed out that premed students tend to be obsessed by getting A's, above all else. Accordingly, they become overachieving, excessively competitive, cynical, dehumanized, and overspecialized (not exactly the qualities you want in someone who is about to make an important decision about your health). These characteristics, the study found, have created an antiscientific attitude among non-premed students, who viewed the premeds as unpleasantly competitive colleagues. To illustrate the pressures of the premed program, the authors referred to a bit of med-school humor. Professor A: "How are things in organic chemistry?" Professor B: "Average, two attempted suicides." Among the many reforms suggested in the report, it was suggested that the MCAT admission test should be abolished since it does not test aptitude, but information retention.

As disturbing as their study may be to some, the fact that Harvard Medical School is willing to consider such changes is an encouraging step toward achieving a whole-brained approach. But as reform begins to take shape at the medical school, what has happened at business schools?

Theodore Levitt, though himself a professor at Harvard Business School, is concerned that America's corporate management is being increasingly taken over by analytic, systematic thinkers such as those produced by our business schools. According to Levitt, "Experts, trained to the teeth in the techniques, are enlisted to do even better what people of native shrewdness, sound good sense, and abundant energy did quite well before."

Professor Michael Porter, whose course in competitive and industrial analysis is reportedly the most popular at the Harvard Business School, stated that, "I thought there had to be a way to make the process of determining strengths and weaknesses, threats and opportunities, more analytical, *so we don't have to rely so much on the vision of the managers."* Despite Levitt's concern and the questionable success of Baker Scholars, Professor Porter and other MBA educators continue to emphasize analytic thinking way ahead of whatever is second. By stressing symbolic, systematic treatment of a rapidly changing world, they are falling into the classic trap of making fixity out of flux.

Our business schools have become so analytic that one wonders whether MBA stands for "Management By Analysis." What is needed is a whole-brained approach. Specifically:

□ Courses need to be taught on creativity in order to teach students how to make interconnections of information from diverse sources as well as how to deal with unique situations. (Creativity is being successfully "taught" at many seminars. There is no reason why those techniques cannot be adopted in the classroom.)

☐ Case studies should be filmed and put on videotape. Since body language and tonal expressions are a greater part of communication than literal meaning, it seems absurd to offer students written cases that deal only with the lesser form of human interaction.

☐ While in school, if it is not already required, MBAs should continually and critically read the *Wall Street Journal* and other publications to get a feel for what is happening in the real world of business. As it is, students are asked to deal almost totally in theory that is based on past realities. As Peter Drucker stated, "When a subject becomes obsolete, we make it a required course."

☐ Writing and other courses should be taught by using methods similar to those used in Betty Edwards's book *Drawing on the Right Side of the Brain* and Gabrielle Rico's *Writing the Natural Way*. The latter book should be particularly valuable as a guide for helping MBAs to learn how to release their expressive writing powers through the use of right-brain techniques.

☐ Students should be selected with less priority given to standard test scores or IQ measurements. These tests are strongly biased in that they are only an indicator of left-hemispheric reasoning ability. As a result, they discriminate against intuitive right-hemispheric skills and tend to create a like-minded student body that can reason brilliantly, but which lacks creativity.

The author recently visited his old MBA alma mater, Northwestern University, and talked with its head, Dean Donald P. Jacobs. When the dean pointed out that their average student had scored 94 percent in the business boards, the author exclaimed with dismay that, if he applied now, his board scores would exclude him from being accepted as a student. To which Dean Jacobs stated, "Don't worry, I couldn't get in either!" One wonders what percent of our country's CEOs would also be excluded.

The shift from the Cognitive Era to the Visual Age will put the educational system under increasing pressure to change. To reverse the process so that cocoons will hatch into butterflies is perhaps the biggest challenge facing Western society. Perhaps it is time to elect Lao Tsu to the board of education!

6

THE LOSER'S GAME

When men do not have a sense of awe, there will be disaster.
—LAO TSU

Nothing is more suicidal than a rational investment policy in an irrational world.
—JOHN MAYNARD KEYNES

History shows that the *Titanic*'s captain was concerned about icebergs, for during the night he stationed two seamen on the bow as lookouts. A few hours before the accident, the *Titanic* received a telegram warning of heavy pack ice and frequent icebergs from the *Carpathian*, a freighter steaming toward the *Titanic*. Unfortunately, this important report became lost among the many telegrams of the passengers and never reached the captain. Shortly thereafter, the two alert lookouts spotted the iceberg and immediately warned the captain, who promptly took proper evasive action. Though the captain's system was operative, its important lack of lead time resulted in one of the most famous marine disasters of all time. By the time the iceberg could be seen, it was too late to be avoided.

The *Titanic's* demise is a classic example of a "loser's game," since the captain's system of spotting icebergs was doomed to failure. On Wall Street similar disasters are repeated over and over each time analysts are "surprised" by an unexpected earnings report. When a "bad quarter" or some other event is reported, Wall Street's electronic communications system spreads the information to everyone, making it impossible to avoid its impact. This scenario is similar to the "Businessman's Catch-22," in which all information must be analyzed. Of course, by the time the numbers are in and the analysis complete, it is often too late; the horse has already left the barn.

The disaster of the *Titanic* was partly the result of the captain's preference for hard, empirical evidence (i.e., seeing an iceberg) as opposed to soft information (clues). For example, the telegram from the *Carpathian* was soft information, a clue that there might be trouble ahead. The sighting of the iceberg was hard information, empirical evidence of trouble. The *Titanic's* captain had taken great pains to set up a system for handling the hard empirical evidence, while neglecting to train his telegraph operator to pass on any input that might give him soft clues about his ship's course.

A contributing factor to the ship's demise was an overload of information. The warning telegram about icebergs had been mixed in with the passengers' less important messages. Had the telegram not been lost and had the captain stressed the importance of such soft information to his operators, the *Titanic* might now be exhibited at the

South Street Seaport Museum (located within a few blocks of Wall Street).

"The Loser's Game," an article by Charles D. Ellis, appeared in the July/August 1975 issue of the *Financial Analysts Journal*. In this article, Mr. Ellis pointed out that professional investors now control 70 percent of the trading volume on the New York Stock Exchange (up from the 1960s' 30 percent). As a result, according to Ellis, the professional investor had become so competitive that almost no one could win. This well-written article certainly seemed to hit the nail on the head, for not only did it receive instant acclaim within the investment community, but its wisdom has held up over time; most professional money managers have continued to underperform the market.

Why can't Wall Street play a "winner's game"? Why can't "the best and the brightest" from our MBA programs who flock to Wall Street figure out how to win? What are the common mistakes that professional investors make? Though radar has solved the iceberg problem for ships, few people have yet devised a methodology for avoiding investment surprises.

The prudent man rule states that, in order to be prudent, one should follow what other men of prudence are doing. There may be times when this principle is appropriate, but it fails to work when the participants watch the actions of each other and then become inappropriately secure in following each other. The Du Pont-Conoco merger in 1981 and the behavior of trout in the following story illustrate "the prudent man's loser's game."

A twelve-year-old was once invited to try his luck at a trout pond that was famous in its Michigan county. One hundred yards long, twenty yards wide, and three feet deep, this pond was loaded with rainbow and brown trout that ranged in size up to eight pounds. Its owner, a friend of the boy's father, smugly challenged the lad to catch as many as he could, knowing that the fish were amply fed with pellet food and that even the most skilled trout fisherman had come up empty trying to tempt these prize trophies.

Thinking he was given a sneak preview of heaven, the boy ran down to the pond to pull in the spoils. Six hours later he understood the reason for the owner's smugness. He had tried dry flies, spinners, flatfish, minnows, worms, and even live frogs—all to no avail. Acting out of frustration, he threw most of his worms into the pond, and sat on the bank watching their snaking motions on the pond's floor.

For ten minutes, the trout watched warily. Then one small fish ate a small worm. Ten more minutes went by and then another small trout gulped down a slightly larger worm. Finally, after another five minutes, a *big* trout took a worm. The fish, feeling safe with the endorsement of one of the biggies, within seconds had transformed the pond into churning white water as it was every trout for himself. With a worm on the boy's hook, it was a slaughter, as the trout now operated under the illusion of safety. The boy soon stood proudly in front of the owner's door with a string of fifteen three-to-five-pounders. Somehow his father's friendship with this man was never quite the same.

In the summer of 1981, the acquisition waters were aswirl over Conoco, with Seagram, Mobil, and Du Pont offering billions upon billions to tempt Conoco's stockholders. But why was this frenzy occurring in the summer of '81? The energy crisis had developed in 1973, eight years earlier. Were the managements of these companies just now beginning to feel that energy might be a good business to be in?

And why, after eight years, did they all seemingly come to the same conclusion within a matter of a few days?

Impressed by the speed with which Du Pont moved during the Conoco acquisition maneuvering, *Chemical Week* magazine, on August 5, 1981, featured an article entitled "When Strategic Planning Pays Off." This article praised Du Pont for demonstrating "the usefulness of its strategic planning system in rapid-fire decision-making."

As it turned out, *Chemical Week*'s eulogy was more akin to congratulating Caesar on the ides of March for his fine speech before leaving the Forum. In feeling secure because the other biggies were trying to eat the worms, Du Pont ended up being caught short by a changing trend. By focusing on the competition of the other players during the feeding frenzy, Du Pont missed reading the many soft indicators available at the time, which indicated that an oil glut was in the making.

There were other reasons why Du Pont was playing a loser's game. With 25,000 professional managers in their employ, Du Pont certainly had spent many man-hours studying the energy area, after the 1973 embargo made energy an important subject. They more than likely consulted with the leading experts on energy. Unfortunately for Du Pont, it is axiomatic that just before a trend changes, there will be maximum agreement by experts and others that the trend will not end! By relying on analytically derived forecasts of the left brain, the right-brained sensing becomes overpowered. If he could, Lao Tsu would interject that Du Pont, by consulting men of knowledge, ended up with the wrong feel of reality for their decision-makers. Their regression analysis and economic models of the price of oil caused them to mistake the symbol for reality. In turn, a false sense of security was created when man once again preferred the artificial and complicated to the simple ways of nature.

THE TOO-LITTLE AND TOO-MUCH OF INFORMATION

Decision-making by investors and managers is least effective when information exists in extremes, when there is either too little or too much.

In a feature article on May 5, 1982, the *Wall Street Journal* did an autopsy of past oil-price forecasting. The inaccuracy of these forecasts was disturbing, especially considering the point made in the article by Rep. Albert Gore of Tennessee that "billions and billions of dollars in private and federal funds are gambled on the basis of forecasts." According to Dennis O'Brien of the U.S. Department of Energy, "All forecasts, both in the government and the private sector, have been awful at figuring out where the energy markets were headed the past few years."

Stephen McNees of the Federal Reserve Bank of Boston added an interesting perspective to this loser's game by stating in the article that forecasters, faced with so much uncertainty, have "clustered together like a herd of sheep." A Taoist would say, "They were but men huddling together and shouting to give themselves courage in the dark."

Man is extremely uncomfortable with uncertainty. To deal with his discomfort, man tends to create a false sense of security by substituting certainty for uncertainty. It becomes the herd instinct. The irony is that the greater the uncertainty, the greater the similarity of predictions, as the experts "shout together in the dark." In turn, the greater will be the collective surprise when their predictions miss the mark. The less information there is available about reality, oftentimes the more uniform the "conventional wisdom" will be.

It is amazing how easily people's opinions are drawn together under conditions of uncertainty. Sadly, many businessmen, despite having made disastrous decisions by following the conventional wisdom, retain their jobs because their files are stuffed with research reports ("How could you expect me to disagree with the 'world's smartest men'?"), and because almost everyone else was wrong as well. And so it goes, as the experts continue to substitute certainty for uncertainty and thus become the losers in the forecasting game.

Eric Ridder, editor of the *Journal of Commerce*, pointed out in an interesting editorial that back in the days of sailing ships, passengers who were light sleepers could adjust to the ship's tacking. Heavy sleepers who could not adjust woke up in the morning with their heads beneath their feet—a sure way to develop a headache. As Mr. Ridder stated, "We don't think it is enough for businessmen to sleep through changing conditions only to waken to the significance of them when everybody else is also awakening to them simultaneously."

When forecasters have too much information, they often become even more inaccurate than when there is too little. Research on horse handicappers and other studies indicate that only early information affects one's decisions. Once the decision is made, additional information, even when contradictory, will not cause the person to change his mind. In fact, as more and more information becomes available, it only reinforces his belief. Additional information does not increase the quality of decision-making, only the certainty of conviction. It only adds a false sense of security.

The Continental Illinois Bank provides another example of disastrous forecasting of the oil picture. One could sense they were prone to playing a loser's game by reading a *Wall Street Journal* article on September 18, 1981, called "In the Highflying Field of Energy Finance, Continental Illinois Bank Is Striking It Rich." In the article, John Redding, senior V.P. of the bank's oil and gas group, boasted that their aggressive lending policy had paid off, as 15 percent of their $4 billion loan portfolio consisted of holdings of independent energy companies. Mr. Redding, secure in the fact that the bank had fourteen petroleum engineers on its staff, confidently told readers that the "current drop in oil prices is just a dip."

Secure in the knowledge that Mexico had lots of oil, and that the need for oil and its price could only go up, the nine largest U.S. banks had loaned 40 percent of their capital to Mexico by 1982. When Mexico began to teeter on the brink of default, many began to question why the bankers had put so many eggs in one basket. This was another case not only of faulty forecasting, but also of the prudent man rule in action. Since all the bankers were competing to get Mexican loans, they concentrated, like the trout in the boy's pond, on outmaneuvering the competition to get the worms. In doing so, they overlooked other aspects of the situation—such as the fact that some of the worms had hooks in them.

While the loser's game in oil forecasting affected many large organizations, it also hurt many individuals. During the abrupt stock market rally of 1982, relatively few individual investors were bullish. Why? In part, because so many had been badly burned in energy stocks. Consider a letter this author received in January 1982: "The whole problem is my naive investment in energy stocks, which faced me with a tragedy. In December 1980, I invested almost $25,000 in energy stocks. At the present time that amount is reduced to $6,000. I don't have enough time to get sources and read and speculate about the energy stocks. I need help." The irony was that he was again doing what had caused his mistake in the first place—looking to someone else to make investment decisions for him. Had he looked at the world around him and noticed smaller cars, lower thermostat settings, and so forth, the outcome might have been different.

INNER SPORTS

As Lao Tsu said, "Certain ends are best accomplished without the use of conscious means." Tim Gallwey made the same discovery and shared his insights with readers in his book *The Inner Game of Tennis.* Gallwey's inspiration for his famous book first developed when he observed a player talking to himself on the tennis court as if there were two people in one body. After further observations, Gallwey concluded that the conscious mind of many players constantly blamed the unconscious mind for a poor performance. He further observed that the more a player berated himself, the more his natural flow was affected and the worse he played.

Gallwey described one incident where he was giving lessons to a group of novice players. In giving them a drill for net play, he asked them to concentrate on their footwork as they returned the shots he hit to them. After the drill, he commented on how well they had done, pointing out that the balls they had hit were clustered in the rear corners of the court, just where they should be. He then asked the group to repeat the drill and again to concentrate on their footwork. The results of this exercise were quite different, as the balls were scattered all over the court, many of them not clearing the net. In the second drill, the students' conscious minds, thinking shot placement, had interfered with their natural flow.

Though Gallwey does not refer directly to the left and right brains in his book, the dual mentality of tennis players is the book's primary focus. By trying to overpower the nonverbal right hemisphere, whose natural province is spatial relationships, players often let the wrong mind dominate the task. The expression "playing out of one's mind" in effect refers to play where the logical, verbal mind is stilled so that the right hemisphere can be in control. (Note: In jogging, that "runner's high" occurs when the blood flow first switches in greater proportion to the right brain, usually ten minutes after starting.) In like fashion, those who can verbalize the techniques and methodologies of a sport tend to be those whose play is least skillful. As Lao Tsu observed, "The man who struggles to carve a piece of jade will mar it, but if he lets his hands guide themselves, the work is easy and perfect."

In golf the conscious mind plays a greater role than in tennis. In *The New Golf Mind*, Dick Coop and Gary Wiren refer to the left hemisphere as the "analyzer" and the right as the "integrator." When one prepares to take a shot, he or she needs to use the analyzer to select the club, measure the wind direction, determine the strategy, etc. Once addressing the ball, however, one needs to turn off the analyzer and switch on the integrator. To do so, the authors suggest previsualizing the shot so as to get the right hemisphere and the body into the flow of the shot.

Bad shots, the book reasons, tend to be the result of either faulty analysis before the swing or inappropriate interference during the swing by the left hemisphere, as when it suggests something like "don't look up" or "don't go into the water." Much like saying a mantra to occupy the left brain during meditation, one lady pro has "ooompah" lettered on the top of her driver to remind her to say this word slowly during her swing. By so occupying her analyzer, her integrator is better able to retain control. In golf, like investing, one ends up playing a loser's game when the wrong hemispheric tool is used for the task.

HEMISPHERIC INVESTING

Just as in golf, it is important when investing in the stock market to use the correct hemisphere. In the first chapter, investing was likened to poker in that both have table talk (what company management is saying), upcards (known statistics and other information about the company's past), and downcards (information that is restricted or unknown).

The task of dealing with the verbal utterances of managers and statistical data is clearly best performed by the analyzer. Unknown or restricted information, on the other hand, is best dealt with by the "Lao Tsu" right hemisphere. Because the dominant method of Wall Street analysts is left brained, the unknown variables are often dealt with poorly or conveniently ignored.

Since logic thrives on cause and effect, analytic thinkers often confuse coincidence with causality. One by-product of the analyzer's need for causality can be seen daily when commentators review the day's stock market trend. If the Dow was down $6.60 on Monday, reporters might say, "The market sold off on renewed fears by investors of higher interest rates." Then on Tuesday, when the market closed up $5.28, the same commentators might well state, "The market was up on hopes of lower interest rates." Of course, the market was up or down because of a variety of interrelated factors that were too complex, diffuse, and intangible to be easily identified. Nonetheless, investors, inappropriately secure in knowing why the market did what it did for the day, could then rest easier that night.

The rate of world change continues to increase. The stock market, as a mirror of global developments, has

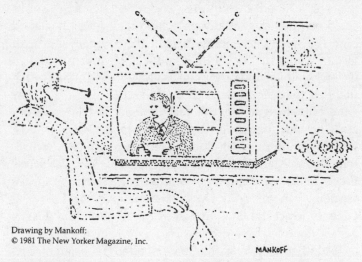

Drawing by Mankoff:
© 1981 The New Yorker Magazine, Inc.

MANKOFF

"On Wall Street today, news of lower interest rates sent the stock market up, but then the expectation that these rates would be inflationary sent the market down, until the realization that lower rates might stimulate the sluggish economy pushed the market up, before it ultimately went down on fears that an overheated economy would lead to a reimposition of higher interest rates."

become more and more characterized by volatility. By trying to analyze such rapid change, one is using the analyzer or left brain to do inappropriately what is better suited to the integrator or right brain, which can see, sense, and feel new developments. By waiting for these developments to be analyzable, one will inevitably be measuring events after the fact, a sure way to play the loser's game. By trying to understand running water by catching it in a bucket, one is doomed to be left behind.

Billions of dollars were lost in 1974 when the "nifty fifty" collapsed. The "nifty fifty" were a group of stocks that had accumulated impressive records of sustained earnings growth. These companies, as a result of their past achievements, satisfied the investment criteria of almost all major investment institutions. Such "one decision" stocks could be purchased at any price (and they certainly all had high P/E ratios), as sooner or later the company's growth factors would make you look good. Such strategy worked well for a while, and certain institutions smiled smugly each night as they slipped into a deep, secure sleep. But they were blithely ignoring the fact that no sizable company could sustain fast enough growth rates to justify such ratios. In doing so, these institutions proved once again the maxim that Burton Malkiel, in his book *A Random Walk Down Wall Street*, refers to: "Stupidity well packaged can sound like wisdom." In his book, Malkiel developed the following table to depict the final outcome of the "nifty fifty" loser's game.

Another loser's game that is often repeated occurs routinely in doctors' offices. Medical students, as we have seen, are selected primarily on the basis of high marks and test results (strong left-hemispheric skills). They are then

SECURITY	PRICE/EARNINGS MULTIPLE 1972	PRICE/EARNINGS MULTIPLE 1980
Sony	92	17
Polaroid	90	16
McDonald's	83	9
International Flavors	81	12
Walt Disney	76	11
Hewlett-Packard	65	18

subjected to training that crams knowledge into their left brain, at the expense of right-side development. As a result, they often miss sensing, seeing, or otherwise feeling the subtle clues best noticed by the "other" hemisphere. These clues, if properly spotted in the early stages, could result in patients being much more effectively treated. How often have doctors stated, "Chances are it is nothing to worry about"? They are usually right, since their diagnosis has a high percentage chance of being correct. However, by definition, in playing the percentages, they risk missing cancer or some other serious disease, which will thus remain undetected until it is too late. In business and investing, as in medicine, the importance of early identification can be depicted by the following model:

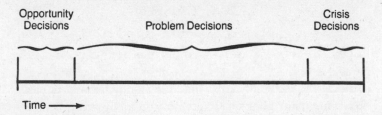

The chart above, plus the stories of energy forecasting

CROCK

CROCK by Bill Rechin and Don Wilder;
© 1981 Field Enterprises, Inc.

and the "nifty fifty," all depict what Shakespeare figured out centuries ago—the difference between a tragedy and a comedy. A comedy is when the characters discover reality in time to do something about it; a tragedy is when the characters do not. Poor Othello, like the leaders of our automotive industry and the investors who owned their stocks, repeatedly ignored the numerous warning signs of impending disaster.

BEATING YOURSELF

In the book *Extraordinary Tennis for the Ordinary Tennis Player*, Dr. Simon Ramo points out that tennis is not one game but two: that the game played by the professionals is strategically different from that played by amateurs. By observing many matches, Ramo noticed that in professional matches, 80 percent of the points were won through winning hits. Thus, the victor was the one who "won" the most

by Bill Rechin & Don Wilder

Courtesy of Field Newspaper Syndicate

points. With amateurs, however, the reverse was true, as 80 percent of the points were lost by whichever player first made a mistake. Therefore, Ramo concluded, in amateur tennis one's strategy for winning should be to avoid mistakes. To play a winner's game, one should avoid trying too hard. As Lao Tsu pointed out, "In making furniture, the more you carve the wood, the weaker it gets."

During the last decade not only did U.S. management frequently not win, it too often lost embarrassingly, as the popularity of books on Japanese management suggests. Though there are many theories as to why our managers have lost to the competition, it all boils down to one basic ingredient—our managerial decision-making has all too often been inferior. How could this happen? After all, just ten years ago we were considered number one—the "best." We had an outright lead in computer technology, the largest number of economists and other experts, and expanding MBA programs. On paper, we looked invincible.

The inescapable answer is that we lost not despite but *because* of our increasingly sophisticated managerial science. Our MBAs, experts, and computer specialists, like the typical amateur tennis player, tried too hard and "marred the jade." In the process they created an overload of information that obscured the vision of business decision-makers and detracted from their seeing reality.

If Lao Tsu were observing these experts in action, he would likely muse on man's tendency to wade into the stream and flail in all directions. By being constantly involved in the desperate fulfillment of activity, man feels that he is alive (even though the stress may shorten his life).

By relying too much on MBAs and other technocrats, Wall Street and corporate America have tipped the managerial balance heavily toward the left brain. As a result, they are playing a loser's game; they are relying on the wrong brain hemisphere for the task of understanding a changing world. Sure, the left brain, like the "world's smartest man," thinks it can do the job, with its theoretical rankings, its sophisticated models that project the past into the future, and its verbal skills to convince us of its infallibility. But t constantly plays the loser's game by trying to make fixity out of flux. As John Maynard Keynes said, "Nothing is more suicidal than a rational investment policy in an irrational world."

7

THE EYES HAVE IT

The more stuffed the mind is with knowledge, the less able one can see what's in front of him.
—LAO TSU

Where there is no vision, the people will perish.
—PROVERBS 29:18

To avoid playing a loser's game, it is essential to use the "right" brain to see reality in time to avoid tragedy. Considering the dynamic pace of world change and the dominance of left-hemispheric expertise, this is not easy to do—though the goal is a simple one.

Sperry Rand Corporation in its advertising campaign advocates being a "good listener." As important as good listening may be, in investing it can be dangerous, because the source of information is experts whose opinions tend to be analytically derived. Even though the column inside the back page of the *Wall Street Journal* is called "Heard on the Street" (it should be called "Herd on the Street"), it should rather be "Seen in the World," for we have to learn to *see* as well as hear.

Since vision is the most information rich of all senses, visual thinking is extremely important and powerful. Accordingly, people's recall of pictures is much greater than that of words. Studies show that one's ability to recall pictures after a week is greater than the ability to remember abstract words after only five minutes! Moreover, you just can't defect from an insight; you can't unsee what you've seen.

In the East, reality tends to be sensed more directly than it is in the West. The two views can be historically contrasted by looking at what happened during the Middle Ages when an unusual event occurred—say, a rooster laying an egg. In the West, history reports that such a genetically confused rooster would be regarded as possessed and would be executed. In the East, the people would gather around and ask what the emperor was doing wrong. One society eliminated the unusual, while the other was motivated to ask questions as to what it indicated.

This tendency of the West to "execute" events that do not fit its dominant belief system (i.e., to pick out only the information that fits one's predetermined viewpoint) is dangerous, as it denies possible clues that change may be occurring. As Einstein said, "Theory shapes the observation." Therefore, the common expression "seeing is believing" is perhaps one of the West's most inaccurate platitudes. In reality, we are much more likely to see what we believe. As Shakespeare's Macbeth asked, "Are my eyes but fools for my other senses?"

Most of our personal, business, and investment problems are not caused because we lack intelligence or are lazy. Rather, the most common cause of failure is that we fail to see and/or otherwise ignore the numerous yellow and red warning signals that are waved before our eyes. Why do we so often miss them?

One reason is that the warning signals are but one of many information inputs vying for our attention. Sociologists calculate that Western man receives 65,000 more stimuli per day than his forebears did one hundred years ago. Investment research reports piled high on the desks of professional investment managers attest to the now-famous overload of information.

Another reason why we see reality so poorly, and so often miss the warning signs, is that our logical left hemisphere interferes with the seeing abilities of the right brain. The following tests are provided to demonstrate this point.

THE "F" TEST

Read carefully the sentence below and count the number of f's in the sentence. Reread it again, carefully:

```
FINISHED FILES ARE THE RE-
SULT OF YEARS OF SCIENTIF-
IC STUDY COMBINED WITH THE
EXPERIENCE OF MANY YEARS.
```

Did you find all six f's? If not, don't be surprised, as only 15 percent of those who take this test get the correct answer. If you counted less than six (most count three), read the same sentence below as it is written backward:

> DEHSINIF SELIF ERA EHT TL-
> USER FO SRAEY FO CIFITNEI-
> CS YDUTS DENIBMOC HTIW EHT
> ECNEIREPXE FO YNAM SRAEY.

By now you have probably realized that you missed the f's in the "of's." Why? Your error was not that you did not see the f's in the of's (you did), but that you failed to count them. Since "of" is phonetically "ov," the verbal left hemisphere, by taking the verbal clue, overrode the right, "seeing" hemisphere and thus forced the wrong conclusion.

Another visual test is provided in the three-letter word below. Can you read what the word is?

If you are having trouble seeing the above word (it is a negative space lettering), try the more filled-in version below.

In order to extrapolate what is missing, you need to use the right hemisphere, as it is by far the one best suited to deal with incomplete information. Most of us, however, try to use our left brains to recognize what is familiar; we are employing the wrong brain half for the task.

To further test your perception, try this "bookworm" test:

BOOKWORM PROBLEM

While this problem looks deceptively simple, it is actually quite difficult. As a matter of fact, only about one person in ten is able to solve it the first time around. There are four volumes of Shakespeare's collected works on the shelf. The pages of each volume are exactly 2" thick. The covers are each 1/6" thick. The bookworm started eating at page 1 of volume I and ate through to the last page of volume IV. What is the distance the bookworm covered?

The answer is five inches. If you had trouble, you were probably trapped by your habitual way of visualizing.

Despite the fact that once you see the answer it is obvious, few persons who take this test get it correct the first time. The left brain is so anxious to get into its mathematical calculations that it pushes aside the initial visual task that the right hemisphere has to perform in order to correctly solve the problem. Positive of its calculations, the left brain volunteers the answer and in the process forces a "half-brained" conclusion. It fails to "see" that the order of the books is different for the worm than it would be for a reader. To read from the first page to the last would mean reading all four volumes, but the bookworm has only to eat through two volumes (including the covers).

Solution—Bookworm Problem

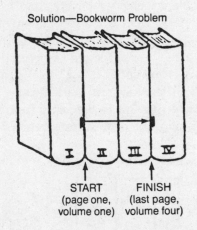

START   FINISH
(page one,   (last page,
volume one)   volume four)

Such an example is illustrative of our Western tendency to carelessness in challenging assumptions. We tend to miss the big picture by jumping too quickly to the details. If the ship's captain in the cartoon survives his impending problem, he might well agree with Lao Tsu's blunt quote, "How stupid to waste our lives in infinite details!"

Well-known psychologist Jerome Bruner conducted an interesting visual test in which he flashed pictures of playing cards on a screen and asked his audience to identify

3-16

DIK BROWNE

HAGAR

them. After a while, he mixed in with the ordinary cards a *red* ace of spades, a *black* five of diamonds, etc. Rather than spot the anomalous cards, the observers would "correct them" in their minds and improperly report a black ace of spades or a red five of diamonds. The fact that the subjects' assumptions limited their ability to see reality shows once again how we tend to ignore our sensory input when it does not fit our dominant beliefs.

Dr. Robert Ornstein in his book *The Psychology of Consciousness* points out that if one lived a lifetime of being awake only during daylight, he would quite likely treat with skepticism claims by night people that there were stars in the heavens. Furthermore, the harder he would look at the blue sky, the more he would classify night people as "crazies." As Ornstein states, "If an object or sensory input appears which does not fit our categories, we tend to ignore it. Therefore, it is difficult to alter our assumptions even in the face of compelling new evidence." We fail to realize that our consciousness is merely our best guess about reality.

The following Taoist story illustrates how one's assumptions affect perception:

> *Once upon a time*
> *a man whose axe*
> *was missing, suspected*
> *his neighbor's son.*
> *The boy walked*
> *like a thief, looked*
> *like a thief, and spoke*
> *like a thief.*
> *But the man found*
> *his axe while he was*
> *working in the field, and*
> *the next time he saw his*
> *neighbor's son, the boy*
> *walked, looked, and spoke*
> *like any other child.*

DRAWING ON THE RIGHT SIDE OF THE BRAIN

Dr. Betty Edwards's best-selling book, *Drawing on the Right Side of the Brain,* is revolutionizing the way that art is being taught. In her six-week drawing course, the improvement of her students is not gradual, but dramatic.

Her techniques for teaching art serve to turn off the overactive left hemisphere. She points out that the left brain interferes with perception because of its simplistic certainty that, if it can name and categorize something, it need not look carefully. Edwards points out that most children lose their capacity for drawing past the age of nine or ten as they get little help from overly busy teachers who are intent on the three R's. Since a child's hand-eye coordination continues to improve until the age of fifteen or sixteen, it is the student's ability to see reality that is not being developed. Dr. Edwards describes how art can still the chatter of the verbal brain, to enter the realm of relationships, meaningfulness, and wholeness. In short, she discusses art as a discovery process to achieve greater self-awareness. As Lao Tsu would add, "The more stuffed the mind is with knowledge, the less able one can see what's in front of him."

One of Betty Edwards's instructional drawing exercises is to draw a picture upside down. The idea is to "trick" the left brain so that it is unable to categorize the facial components. In a like manner, forgers commonly copy signatures upside down in order to eliminate the bias of their own writing. In reality, we all know how to draw, but old habits of poor seeing interfere with that ability and block it.

"ELEPHANTEYESIS"

The famous story of the blind men touching different parts of the elephant and incorrectly deducing that the beast was a rope, a tree, and a snake makes an important point

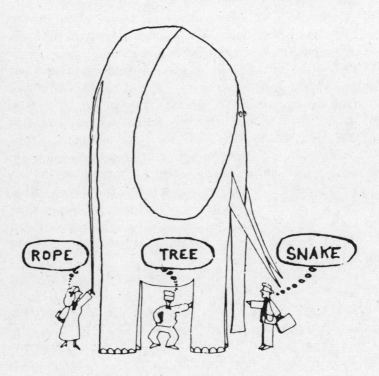

about perception. One cannot get the big picture from a linear sum of independent observations. The following Taoist story illustrates this aspect of perception.

Just before the fox pounced on the plump jackrabbit, he

congratulated himself for having the good fortune to live in a land of plenty. The eagle, as he looked down from a soaring turn, lamented that there was only one rabbit in the whole land, and that it was just about to be eaten by a fox.

Like the fox, experts tend to look at the text of life close up, and often miss the big picture that would be obvious from afar. The basic difference between commonplace and creative solutions is often that the field of vision of the person with creative insight is larger.

Wayne Gretsky is a remarkable hockey player because he is both a prolific scorer and a top assist man. Such a combination of skills is unusual, as the vision of a scorer needs to be focused on the goal, whereas an assist specialist needs to be able to "see" the whole rink so as to know the position of the other players. In this respect, hockey is like the ancient Chinese story of the ox and the cat. Though big and slow, the ox is difficult to catch as he can see anyone approaching and will warily take cover. The cat, though quick and agile, is easily caught in a net for he cannot see someone approaching while he is intently focused on his prey—the mouse.

Like the cat, investors have to continually guard against outfoxing themselves by being overly focused on the near-term promise of a payout. The market is composed of too many variables and is characterized by too much flux to justify a secure, confident attitude. Like so many others, this author has made his worst investment mistakes when he was the most certain about being right, when he lacked the "wisdom of insecurity." H. L. Mencken stated, "There is always an easy solution to every human problem—neat, plausible, and wrong."

Studies of stock market trading patterns indicate that

price movements are 50 percent correlated to general market changes, 35 percent to the movement of industry groups, and only 15 percent to the result of the dynamics of an individual stock. If one focuses like the cat on one issue, he is considering the least important factor of the three main causes of price movement. One might then end up like the fox, wondering where all the rabbits went.

DISCOVERY

Visionaries are not people who see things that are not there, but who see things that others do not see. As Einstein quipped, "Why do some people see the unseen?" (It should be noted that Einstein's "thought experiences" were frequently visual.) But one does not have to be an Einstein to be a discoverer or a visionary; chances are, the greater the idea, the more it came from a basic observation. Thus, in hindsight, the most ingenious discoveries display an embarrassing degree of simplicity. As biologist Thomas Huxley said when he read about Darwin's new theory, "How extremely stupid of me not to have thought of that." Lao Tsu would have been most pleased to learn how many important scientific discoveries were inspired by simple observations of nature.

It is the author's experience that discovery is often accompanied by a thrill, that famous eureka feeling. Quite often, however, the feeling of elation is all too quickly replaced by a feeling of stupidity, as one wonders why it took so long to see the obvious!

Fritz Perls, the father of gestalt psychotherapy, was once visited by a violinist with a problem. For years this man had been the most talented violinist in his orchestra. However, because his skills all but disappeared when he stood up to play solo parts, he had spent years patronizing various psychoanalysts in an effort to solve his problem. On hearing his story, Perls, to the utter dismay of the violinist, sent him home to get his instrument. When the man returned and played for Fritz, he struggled as usual. Perls, however, observed that when the man played, he put his weight primarily on one foot, which resulted in excessive swaying. He advised him to place equal weight on both feet, and the violinist was instantly cured! After investing thousands of dollars and considerable time in analysis, the violinist had his problem solved in only one session by a skillful observer.

In investing in the stock market, it is important to discover or see reality before events can be quantified and then easily identified by the analytic horde. As Marilyn Ferguson said in *The Aquarian Conspiracy*, "Detecting tendencies and patterns is a crucial skill. The more accurately we can get the picture from minimal information, the better equipped we are to survive. The ability to close a pattern with limited information enables the successful retailer or politician to detect trends, the diagnostician to name an illness, the therapist to see an unhealthy pattern."

BODY LANGUAGE

If you listen for literal meaning, you will have a life filled with unpleasant surprises. As the following chart, which summarizes the research findings of Albert Mehrabian, shows, the literal meaning of talk during face-to-face con-

versations is very much the least reliable form of
communication:

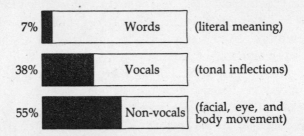

7%	Words	(literal meaning)
38%	Vocals	(tonal inflections)
55%	Non-vocals	(facial, eye, and body movement)

We have long known that what people say is not
necessarily the same as what they do. Most corporate
managers intuitively sense this principle, as they choose to
spend so much time in face-to-face meetings. Rather than
read a plant manager's report about production problems, a
good company president would prefer to meet with him to
see what questions cause him to squirm, to observe his
facial expressions, etc.

There are several books on body language, and as
another bit of evidence of our society's left-brained "analexic" dominance, it is interesting to note that the best-selling
one does not have any pictures or diagrams! Another book,
How to Read a Person Like a Book by Nierenberg and Calero
(Pocket Books) does have illustrations. Since its authors
based their work on the observation of videotapes of management and labor negotiations, the book also has a business orientation.

The author has found this book to be more helpful in
business than any other text (certainly more so than the one
used in Economics 101). A few body patterns that the author
found to be particularly helpful when persuading others to
accept ideas:

SIGN	INDICATOR	RESPONSE	RESULT
Crossed arms	I don't buy what you're saying	Stop talking; ask if there's anything that might be bothering them	Objections are quickly put on the table; by clearing them up early, other person is freer to listen
Hand over mouth or touching ear (a quirk left over from school when raised hand to ask question)	Wants to talk in order to make a point or ask a question	Pause, allow the person to participate	Motiviation of buyer becomes more identifiable
Leans forward	Has reached a decision	Stop talking and start closing	Will avoid talking yourself out of a sale

Body language is an important aspect of business, as success is often dependent on the ability to see through human interactions and discover covert meanings and motives. As an old Cantonese proverb states, "Watch out for the man whose stomach doesn't move when he laughs."

Seeing is not just looking, but the capacity to understand something at once. If you see what is meant, you have an intuitive, right-brained, "Lao Tsu" grasp of things. As Lao Tsu stated, "The power of intuitive understanding will protect you from harm until the end of your days." In other words, it will keep you from playing losers' games.

8

ELEMENTARY, WATSON

Take care of what is difficult while it is still easy, and deal with what will become big while it is yet small.
—LAO TSU

Good intelligence is nine-tenths of any battle.
—NAPOLEON

After ordering his troops to stop their advance and dig in, General Patton inspected the front lines. Something unusual caught his eye—there were cart tracks in the snow where the Germans had picked up their dead and wounded from the battlefield. Patton inferred that this avoidance of motorized vehicles by the Germans indicated a lack of gasoline. Sensing an advantage, Patton ordered his troops forward and, as a result, significantly shortened the war.

The above story is an example of inferential reasoning. According to Webster's, to infer is to arrive at a decision or opinion by reasoning from known facts or evidence (e.g., from your smile, I infer that you're pleased). An inference can also be a matter of making connections between events that are not obviously related. General Patton observed the anomaly of cart tracks and made the connection that the Germans were low on gas—a rather creative and important leap.

Undoubtedly the most renowned inferrer of all times was Sherlock Holmes. He was a master at spotting anomalies (clues) and making creative connections in order to solve the mystery. In one of his cases, Sherlock Holmes inferred that the killer and the victim knew each other very well because of the actions of a dog. Mystified, Watson asked how the dog helped solve the crime. Elementary, Holmes replied; since the neighbors did not hear the dog bark, the dog must have been familiar with the murderer, which would happen only if the murderer had frequently visited the victim's home.

Sir Arthur Conan Doyle derived the Sherlock Holmes method from his mentor, the great Edinburgh diagnostician Joseph Bell. Before the crime can be solved or the patient cured, one has to see the symptoms or clues and then deduce the relevant circumstances. In the case of medicine, it is interesting that there is mounting criticism of the ability of doctors to properly "see," which is the key to a diagnostician's skill. It appears that, by overrelying on expensive laboratory testing, their ability to size up a patient's condition intuitively has severely atrophied.

As a modern-day Sherlock Holmes, Columbo has entertained TV audiences with his favorite comment when seeing an anomaly, "This bothers me." In one episode, what bothered Columbo was a bullet hole. He observed that it entered the victim's coat two inches below where it entered the body. Columbo inferred that the two-inch difference was best explained by the victim's having his hands in the air in a surrendering gesture when he was shot. In Columbo's eyes, this made the murderer's plea of self-defense look extremely suspect.

The fact that the CIA practices inferential reading on a continuous basis (they call inferences "reduced cues") is demonstrated by an interesting story. Several years ago an agent who monitored Russian newspapers at the CIA noticed an anomaly: A small town's soccer team, which was the perennial last-place team, suddenly began winning their games by lopsided scores. Intrigued, the reader persuaded the agency to fly a U-2 plane over the town to take detailed photographic mapping. These pictures revealed that a well-camouflaged military installation had been built in the town. Though the Russians went out of their way to hide the plant, they didn't realize that the technicians imported to manage the facilities would improve the town's soccer team. This unintended message proved to be a clue to the new reality.

In a 1977 *New York Times* article, a U.S. government official who was touring a Nissan motor plant was reported as remarking, "It's a quarter to eleven, what a strange time for the workers to take a break." As it turned out, the workers were not taking a break, because the workers were robots! After musing over the official's naivete, I began to probe the significance of the robotic developments in Japan along with my three partners. Our further investigation indicated that robots had given Japanese auto companies a decided advantage over Detroit, who had resisted the new technology. Robots were cheaper (the largest cost of making a U.S. car

other than direct labor is the health care of the workers), better (weld tolerances for robots are twice as accurate as for
humans), and more flexible (model-year styling could be
changed by reprogramming, at 15 percent of the cost of
retooling).

Armed with these observations, we were able to infer
that Detroit was in trouble, whereas Cincinnati Milacron
and Condec, who manufactured robots, had good opportunities to sell their products to "The Big Three" when they
finally woke up to what the Japanese were doing (these
stocks subsequently went up two to three times). Later, by
seeing the new Japanese cars, the public was also able to see
the results of the Japanese robot advantage, as their cars
were cheaper, more stylish, better constructed, and able to
get better mileage. Our automotive managements seemed
to be the last to admit the new reality.

THE WINDOW OF OPPORTUNITY

Lao Tsu pointed out that "when things reach maturity,
they decay of themselves." As the rate of change increases,
a la *Future Shock*, things reach maturity and then decay at an
increasing pace. Though the oil opportunity for investors
lasted only between 1973 and 1980, it was longer than the
five-year "window of opportunity" for most new business
fields.

The narrowing of the window of opportunity increases
the responsibility of corporate management to practice good
timing. There is an ever-greater need to identify opportunities in the early stages as well as sense when to sell or
quit the business while others are still enthusiastic about its
potential. To fit within the window of opportunity, corpora-

tions are forced to try to hit a moving target. As a result, investing in stocks today is akin to hitting a moving target that, in turn, is trying to hit a moving target.

In Chapter 1, investing was compared with poker, with its table talk (what management will say about its business), upcards (statistical measurements of the past), and downcards (restricted or unknown information). Though upcards and table talk are extensively followed by security analysts, the downcards tend to be ignored or merely guessed at, since they cannot be analyzed. Nor can the early "straws in the wind" that indicate changing conditions be analyzed. However, they can often be sensed, through the kind of inferential discipline practiced by Sherlock Holmes.

THE CEO'S CIA

A crisis can be defined as a severe change. It is interesting that the Chinese do not have a word for crisis. What they do have, however, is a two-word idiom: crisis equals danger and opportunity. It is the purpose of Inferential Focus, the author's firm, to identify these dangers and opportunities before they can be proven by statistical measurements (i.e., analyzed).

The original inspiration for IF's methodology came from a veterinarian, Dr. Chick Carniglia of Suffield, Connecticut. Over fifteen years ago Dr. Carniglia noticed that the toenails on one foot of a German shepherd were longer than those on the opposite foot. Though the dog's walk was normal, the veterinarian insisted on having the leg with the long toenails X-rayed, and this revealed a vertical fracture. Though the injury was not noticeable when the dog walked, a clue to the problem was provided by the foot with the long nails (the nails on the other foot had been worn down when the dog was digging).

What methodology does Inferential Focus employ to identify the early indicators of change? IF's discipline centers on the reading of 180 publications, which range from *Adhesive Age* to *Yankee* (many of these subscriptions are trade periodicals). Such reading serves as a "radar screen" on which the anomalies, or clues of change, first appear. This reading also provides a feeling for what is normal, as one needs to know normality in order to recognize an anomaly (something that shouldn't be happening in terms of "conventional wisdom"). When sufficient anomalies or breaks in a trend are noted, IF infers that a new trend is forming.

The early indicators of change often come from outside the area that eventually is most affected (e.g., the Swiss watch industry was nearly mortally surprised by developments in the semiconductor area). Broad-based readings allow one to spot a change in one field that will impact another. Experts, on the other hand, are vulnerable to being surprised by events outside their specialized area. For example, our society is so specialized that there are many trade publications for each field of expertise, which tend to reinforce conventional wisdoms. IF is one of the few organizations to read across the categories so as to be able to sense cross-disciplinary interrelationships.

The inferential process is not analytical, but one of synthesis. The reader starts with a great deal of information and synthesizes or reduces it by separating the wheat from the chaff. By discarding both opinion and what is expected, Lao Tsu's rule of "adhering to the genuine and discarding the superficial" is observed.

The process of spotting change is essentially visual, and is hence the domain of the right brain, as is the creative process of connecting seemingly disparate events. Inferential thinking, however, is very much whole brained; the left brain stores up the knowledge acquired during the reading so as to provide a background against which the right brain can spot anomalies.

INTEGRATING INFERENCE INTO DECISION-MAKING

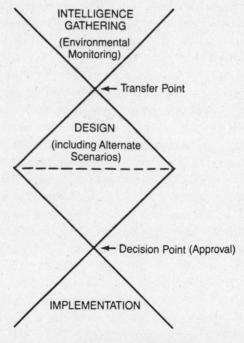

As the above diagram illustrates, there are five stages to the decision-making process: intelligence, information transference, design, approval, and implementation. Intelligence is the process whereby information about competitive, economic, internal factors is synthesized to determine what issues represent dangers and opportunities. The transfer point occurs when management takes the information derived from the intelligence function and decides what needs further investigation (a design function).

Whereas intelligence develops the questions, design activity is an analytic search to find answers and map out possible strategies. Alternatives are explored and research undertaken so that management can be presented with alternatives for a final decision. Once decided upon, of course, the plan is implemented.

The first stage of decision-making, the intelligence process, is the most critical. In corporate strategic planning, it is the process that sets the whole course of decision-making. For investors, it is important not only because it gives them an information time advantage over the analytic community, but also because it gives clues to the general economic and industry-wide trends that correlate historically with 85 percent of the reasons why stocks move.

Discovery is news to be broken, not classified. Therefore, IF centers its communication on monthly verbal dialogue with individuals at client organizations. Often when an inference is made, clients can add their own observations that were made but not connected with change factors. When people are confronted with evidence of change, they will tend not to take the first input seriously—and with good reason, because to do so would cause neurotic instability (as the expression goes, one robin does not make a spring). For an individual to take seriously the possibility of change, he needs to have three to five inputs about the new trend. In fact, this phenomenon is so predictable that IF routinely refers to it as the "Inferential Focus 3 to 5 rule."

IF inferential reasoning has a disadvantage as an investment tool; at times it can be too early. In October 1978 the *Wall Street Journal* in a feature article about the author's group called "Investment Advisers Use Intuition to Challenge Wall Street Views on Major Economic Trends" stated, "The world will have oil for years to come." In support of this view, the article pointed out that a 1.2-million-barrel-per-day oil pipeline was quietly being constructed in Russia (thus the CIA conclusion that the USSR would become a net importer of oil by 1982 was off base, as they actually exported 1.5 million barrels per day for the year) and that giant oil fields were being discovered in Mexico. Yet within a year, the Shah of Iran was overthrown and the price of oil as well as the value of energy stocks soared. It was not until early January 1980 that the glut factor began and energy stocks started their steep decline. IF's correct oil inference about Russia and Mexico was offset by the Shah's downfall. As a result, oil stocks continued to be very good investments in 1978 and 1979.

An example of the integration of inference and decision-making is the "Case of the Saudi Box." A small article that appeared on the second page of the *Wall Street Journal* in October 1979 stated that without warning the Saudis suddenly had changed their shipping requirements on all incoming containerized freight. Conventional containers, which measured forty feet and contained two doors, were now required to be scaled back to just twenty feet and had to have four doors. Not only that, but the Saudis went from inspecting 20 percent of the incoming containers to 100 percent.

Because the Saudis were taking such dramatic action,

they had to be worried about illegal arms shipments, and therefore about the security of their country. One professional investor took this piece of intelligence and mulled it over. He realized that if the Saudis were that concerned, they would switch part of their vast wealth into gold. Following this insight with "design planning" (whether to buy coins, gold mining stocks, or bullion), he decided to buy bullion and bought a sizable holding at $372 per ounce. Six weeks later the Grand Mosque in Mecca was seized by rebels in a revolution attempt that nearly succeeded. What happened to the price of gold? Within three months it soared from $372 to $610 per ounce.

INFERENCE AND YOU

Though IF does not provide its intelligence findings to the general public, its methodology is available to everyone. Mankind, after all, has been making inferences since the time of Adam and Eve. All that is necessary is for one to

FRANK AND ERNEST   Reprinted by permission; © 1979 NEA, Inc.

have a good feel for normality from reading and personal experience. As in understanding the Chicken and the Ark cartoon, all one has to do then is to interconnect observations and knowledge correctly in order to sense future possibilities.

Yes, Watson, the point of the cartoon is elementary. Nonetheless, it is surprising how few people understand the cartoon—even though the alarmed chicken has observed for you the anomaly that there are more chickens than any other animal (one person out of four makes the proper inference regarding the cartoon). Knowing that chickens are food and that humans are carnivorous, our alarmed chicken realized that twenty-five of them would likely be eaten! Statistically he had only a 7.4 percent chance of survival!

Seeing reality and making proper inferences can give you a strategic advantage. However, keep in mind that though inferential reasoning significantly improves the odds, it does not provide a sure bet. The Germans could have fooled Patton by faking cart tracks in the snow; the Russians could have planted artificial soccer scores; and Noah could have brought along the chickens for their egg-laying capabilities. Nonetheless, most great scientific leaps started with inferential insight. Furthermore, in investing one has to sense when the road curves in order to be successful. Such sensing is where anyone with a modicum of common sense can have an advantage over the professional security analysts of Wall Street who time and time again miss the curve in the road as they look into the rearview mirror.

9

TAO INVESTORS

He who knows how to be aggressive, and yet remains patient, becomes a receptacle for all of Nature's lessons.
—LAO TSU

In the investment game risk and returns are inseparable.
—DONALD R. KURTZ,
Equitable Life Assurance Society

In 1973 Jim Rogers, cofounder of the Soros Fund, was puzzled by the outcome of air battles during the Egyptian–Israeli War (which was later called the Six-Day War). Rogers noticed that the Israelis, who had superior pilots and aircraft, were losing the air war to a supposedly inferior Egyptian air force. He inferred that the Egyptian air success was the result of a superiority of electronic weaponry. Moreover, since the Israelis' weapons were supplied by the U.S. and the Egyptians' by Russia, Rogers deduced that Russia had better "smart" electronic weaponry than the United States.

Fascinated by this insight, Rogers looked into defense spending and found that, as a percentage of GNP, defense spending in the U.S. had declined for several years. An interview with the Pentagon revealed that they were well aware of the disadvantage and were pushing for more expenditures for electronics. Finally, a check with Senator Proxmire's office revealed that, though Proxmire was firm about his ongoing crusade to cut overall defense spending, even he realized our need to upgrade our electronic weaponry capability.

Sensing an investment opportunity, Rogers began his "design" research in order to find out which companies would benefit from what seemed to him to be a sure bet—that defense spending for "smart" electronic weaponry would go through the ceiling. Checking within the industry, Rogers found that Lockheed, though a rumored bankruptcy candidate, had "skunk works" (small independent units) that were considered to be the leader in our space program's electronic missiles and other areas too sensitive to talk about. E-Systems and Loral Electronics (selling at two dollars per share and teetering on the brink of bankruptcy) were two other "smart" weapon plays that Rogers bought.

Excited about the possibility of future growth and surprised at the low price of the stocks, the Soros Fund bought heavily. Shortly thereafter, Rogers was visited by two well-known investment fund managers who asked him what he was buying. When Rogers mentioned the "smart weapons" play and the resultant positive pressures for Lockheed and the two other companies, one of his guests turned to the other and commented with a knowing smile, "Who would ever invest in stocks like those?" Rogers responded by buy-ing even more "stocks like those" for his fund.

By 1982 the "smart electronics" stocks were 20 to 50 times the price that Rogers had paid, and Lockheed was a standard fixture at the top of the buy list of even the largest bank trust departments. As for Rogers, after ten years of work with no vacation, he quit the Soros Fund (for which he had been instrumental in engineering a 42-times perfor-mance record increase), cashed in his equity for a reported $14 million, and "retired" at the age of thirty-seven. Though relatively unknown within the Wall Street community, Jim Rogers qualifies as one of the top inferential investors of all time.

When asked the reason for his success, Rogers credits hard work, independent thinking, and insight. Jim certainly worked hard (often fifteen hours a day). In the process, he accumulated a vast filing system from his reading of some forty trade and other publications. He also became familiar with almost all companies traded publicly on the exchanges or over the counter.

As for insight, Rogers merely saw what was beginning to change and capitalized on the future dangers and oppor-tunities the change presented. In order to take advantage of such shifts, he usually held stocks for long periods, confi-dent that his judgment would eventually be rewarded. Though the fund took many positions, Rogers made only ten to twenty major investment plays during the ten years he was associated with it. He was an investor, not a trader, and was interested only in playing changes in major trends.

A case in point is Avon, which had a great track record. Its earnings had increased for thirty years while the company had achieved a fantastic 20 to 30 percent return on equity. The more security analysts projected the past into the future, the higher its price-earnings ratio soared; it frequently sold over 70 times its earnings. Rogers thought of Avon when he began to notice that younger women were going for "the natural look." Women couldn't afford cosmetics during the depression and then couldn't get them during the war. Rogers noticed these factors and realized that Avon had been sailing with the wind behind its back as pent-up demand was being satisfied. Moreover, Avon was facing increased competition as other companies entered the arena in search of promised return on equity. Finally, noting the killer, the natural look, Rogers could not resist and sold Avon short at $130. Within a year the wind had shifted into Avon's face, and Rogers covered his short under $25. (Selling short is the process of selling stock you do not actually own in hopes of earning profits by buying it back later at a lower price.)

What help in his investing did Rogers receive from the members of the *Institutional Investor*'s All-Star Research Team? When asked this question, Rogers asked what the research team was (he had never heard of it)! He added that he had never met an analyst for whom he had any respect. "They all follow the herd, and even when you tell them that things are changing, they not only do not believe you, but will pooh-pooh any evidence you care to point out." He feels analysts are the guys who hold your hand in a most elegant manner while your portfolio continues to lose an average of 3 to 4 percent a year. Rogers makes a point of not reading "Street" research for, since there aren't any Indians, he sees no point in sending for the cavalry.

In 1971 Rogers noticed that natural gas pipelines were

having trouble lining up enough gas to supply their customers. A quick check into the area revealed that federal regulations of natural gas enacted in the early 1950s had kept prices artificially low. In turn, well drilling had declined every year since 1956. Feeling that this trend could not continue, Rogers visited the headquarters of Helmerich and Payne, and Parker Drilling, two companies whose stock prices were severely depressed. When he pointed out what exciting future growth possibilities were in store for the company's drilling services, one drilling executive replied, "You don't understand. The drilling industry is never exciting." In 1973 when OPEC upped the price of oil, the Soros Fund made a killing as the industry became one of the most exciting on Wall Street. Lucky? Not according to Rogers, who felt that supply and demand eventually had to balance out—it was just a matter of how and when. Where are oil prices headed in the next few years? Ten dollars or so a barrel, Rogers predicts, for that is the level where supply and demand factors will align.

Though he often acts contrary to the Street, Rogers does not see himself as a contrary investor. He defines a contrarian as someone who would have bought U.S. Steel every year since 1959. Though he went to Yale and Oxford, he feels that a formal education is of next to no help in making money in the stock market. When he was a trainee at Dominick and Dominick, Rogers did think about going to Harvard to get his MBA. When he asked a senior partner what he thought of the idea, he was advised, "Short beans [selling short soybeans futures] and you'll learn more in just one trade than you would in two years at the 'B School.' " Rogers took his advice without regrets.

By directly observing the world rather than listening to

the analytic scholars, Jim Rogers certainly followed in the footsteps of Lao Tsu. His best investment ideas came from basic observations such as inept pilots winning air battles and women opting for the natural look. And these are ideas that are the province of anyone who can see the "unseen."

ROY NEUBERGER

In an ancient Taoist story, workers stood on the bank and watched with horror as an old man was swept over the falls. They rushed below to see what they could do, only to find the old man calmly sitting on a rock. When asked why he was safe when he could have been killed, the old man said, "Since I grew up with water, I do not think about its flow. I accommodate myself to the water, not the water to me."

During 1982 Roy Neuberger kept testing the flow of the bond market, taking a small loss here and there. The process was repeated several times until things felt right. At this point, he plunged in heavily, placing himself in "Position A" just as the bond market staged one of its most dramatic rallies of all time.

Born in 1903, Roy has been an active market investor for over fifty years and is still a standard fixture in Neuberger & Berman's boardroom. Sensing the flow of the electronic tape with watchful eyes, he takes positions in selected stocks in order to get a better feel for their nature. The timing—when to own major stakes—is a key investment criterion. "Timing is partly intuitive, partly contrary, and requires independent thinking," Roy points out.

Neuberger believes in value, and tries to discover companies before their price-earnings multiple becomes excessive. As he states, "Rarely can securities be valued correctly at over fifteen times earnings, because rarely is there any clear prospect that a company's earnings will grow sufficiently in the future to make it worth that price." Lao Tsu might agree about the unpredictability of the future: "Nature alternates dynamically."

In 1980 Roy focused on a stock that he felt was valued excessively. Schlumberger had a phenomenal earnings record, obtaining a 30 to 40 percent annual growth for several years. Since it had about 293 million shares outstanding at a price of 87, it had a hefty total market evaluation of $25 billion. Feeling that such a price was excessive even if the company continued to show good earnings growth, Roy took the largest short position of his life. The stock obliged, its price declining from 87 to 30. As Roy advises, "Buy when times are hard, and sell when they're good; when it's too easy, move to safety."

When the tax laws were changed several years ago to benefit SBICs (Small Business Investment Companies), Roy began to buy Narragansett Capital (the largest SBIC in the country). Narragansett turned out to be a roller coaster, as its stock went from $4 to almost $40 and back to $4. By then Roy not only liked the stock, but also the company's president, Roy Little (who earlier founded Textron). Neuberger bought heavily and became the second largest stockholder, riding the stock back to about $40. He then kissed his holdings good-bye, sticking to his motto: "Stay in love with a security until the security gets overvalued, then let someone else fall in love."

Roy first spotted Schraffts, the New York City restaurant chain, when it was trading at $4. He kept buying it as it moved to $20, and then bought a substantial block.

This decision turned out to be the worst investment Roy ever made. "I liked to eat at Schraffts and felt that its business was easy to understand." It may have been easy for Roy to understand, but not for its management; the company's fortunes soon took a severe dive.

Aware of his fallibility, as well as the tentative nature of the investment game, Roy follows a policy of taking a loss anytime his investment loses 10 percent of its purchase price. "This creates a reservoir of buying power that can be used to make fresh judgments on what are the best values in the market at that time. The mistake of many is to make one decision and to get locked into that position."

As Lao Tsu avoided the "artificial rules of man," so does Roy Neuberger. A colleague of his likes to tell the story of when he and Roy attended a meeting during the height of the popularity of esoteric electronic stocks. Just as Lao Tsu felt scholars create a barrier of intimidating words in order to sound superior, so did the research analyst who lectured at the meeting. He waxed enthusiastic about the technological wonders of his favorite "black box" stock. Halfway through the presentation, Roy got up to leave, which prompted the scholarly lecturer to ask him why he was not staying. Roy replied, "Just because I don't understand it doesn't mean it's attractive."

One investment Roy could understand is AT&T. In 1958, when its stock was selling at 27, AT&T issued convertible bonds that were AAA rated, yielded 6¼ percent, and had a small conversion premium (i.e., all the features an investor in convertible bonds likes to see). Since the prime lending rate was only 3½ percent, Roy borrowed heavily and bought major positions in the convertible bonds. In the next two years, the common stock rose from 27 to over 70, which greatly benefited the convertible bonds, and Roy then sold the bonds when the stock was between 50 and 60, and realized a 20-times gain on his investment.

"I've used the word 'gut,' but it really is more a matter of sticking to a commonsense viewpoint." Leery of experts, Roy long ago discovered that economists didn't handle their money better than anyone else. He is also leery of economists and others "who predict too much." As for institutional Wall Street research, Roy states, "The greatest game among a number of research firms seems to be to find out the next quarter's earnings before someone else does." Analysts, he finds, tend to overbelieve in growth; as a result, the institutional crowd "sometimes overinfluence each other and are the victims of their own habits."

Though Roy's success is impressive, it is interesting that more of his trades lose money than make profits. The fact that he has a greater percentage of wrong than right is offset by the few investments that turn out to be real winners. Likewise, a highly skilled poker player does not care so much about winning the most pots as he does about the few big ones.

Taoists are known for their old age and young attitudes. Eighty-year-old Roy Neuberger believes that education continues from birth to death. He states, "I'd stop living if I didn't have the opportunity to learn something every day." Such intuition is confirmed by scientific research that shows that in the elderly the physical brain does not lose a measurable number of cells if its environment is stimulating. As the stock market is always changing as well as teaching new lessons, it may be a way to help senior citizens "become more senior."

DON KURTZ—THE QUIET FIGURE BEHIND
$8 BILLION

When the Equitable Life Assurance Society decided in
1959 that they needed common stock management capability, twenty-nine-year-old Donald R. Kurtz was assigned the
responsibility for building the new department. Don had
spent four years in the Navy, two getting his MBA at Co-
lumbia, and two working as a junior analyst in Equitable's
loan department. Since he did not have any investment experience, he set about his assignment with no preconceived
ideas. "The fact that we didn't have a road map and operated with a blank page was instrumental in our success,"
Kurtz states. "Things turned out well because no one had
any preset ideas on how things worked, and thus we were
not locked into procedures, bias, etc."

Such a situation is a rarity for a large organization, a fact
that Kurtz not only recognized at the time, but of which he
took full advantage. Operating on a trial-and-error basis and
with an open mind, he visited many expert investors, and
sorted out what he felt would work and what wouldn't. He
concluded that investing is such a unique, creative, and intuitive process that he needed to establish a personal and
organizational common vision. Such guidelines should be
flexible and allow both communality and individuality to
coexist and flourish. After this was accomplished, Kurtz
states, "We just grew."

At first Don operated with a small staff of three or four.
In 1973, they "went competitive" when they accepted their
first outside money management assignment. By the early
1970s, when Equitable's investment staff of seven was still
relatively small, especially considering that their money

under management totaled $500 million, Kurtz was still making most of the major investment decisions. Kurtz's duties have now changed to administrative ones. This shift was necessitated by the fact that Equitable monies under management have now reached the incredible level of over $8 billion, "every nickel of which is aggressive, active money," Kurtz points out.

Equitable's growth has been remarkable, indeed. Over the last fifteen years, the company has had one of the best, if not the best, performance records of all the large institutional investors. This enviable record, moreover, took place under the tutelage of just one person—one who had no prior investment experience.

Most large investment organizations do well in certain types of markets, but poorly in others. The key difference in their results as compared to Equitable's is that Kurtz's organization flourishes in many different market environments. In the early 1970s Equitable outperformed others by being early in the "nifty fifty" stocks, then making a timely switch to "basic industries." From the late 1970s through the end of 1980, they were heavily positioned in the energy and technology stocks. Feeling that the price of oil had reached a peak and energy conservation was beginning to gain strong momentum, they correctly switched to a disinflationary scenario.

Kurtz refers to his management style as "nonstructured leadership," and readily agrees with Lao Tsu's statement, "Govern a large country as you would cook a small fish—lightly." Kurtz has staffed his organization with people who think the way he does. His thirty staff members are curious, open-minded, flexible, quiet, and low-key. These qualities, Don feels, have to exist naturally as they cannot be taught. He does, however, value an MBA in recruiting, as it shows that the candidate not only has certain technical skills, but has a strong enough belief in himself or herself to invest the time and money to obtain a degree. Kurtz is quick to add that an MBA is no guarantee that one has the intangible qualities he values so highly. He feels that these inner strengths often cannot be predetermined, because they may not show up until someone has been on the job for over two years.

At Equitable, everything is looked at in portfolio terms. Research is focused on the decision-making process, and is not allowed to become an end product in itself, as happens in so many large investment management firms. Kurtz discourages research independence because he feels it can result not only in losing sight of organizational objectives, but also in unwanted competition within.

Don feels that there are two basic types of investment organizations. One kind is like Equitable's, where there are "investors with a capital I." The other kind is technocratically oriented, has rigid, quantifiable rules, and employs techniques designed to limit risks. Kurtz feels this type of organization may be fine for certain types of business, but not for investing, which is so highly dependent on creative and intuitive processes. The worst thing that can (and often does) happen to an investment organization, Don believes, is the appointment of a new investment head who has an excellent track record based on a "system." If such an individual has a big ego, is not flexible, and employs organizational charts and new directives, the creative staff members will be driven out by a sort of Gresham's law and will be replaced by technocrats who will instigate more rules and systems. Investment policy will thus be more and more dominated by individuals who will perfect the art of going wrong with confidence, a sure way to end up in another loser's game.

As Don likes to say, "In the investment game, risk and return are inseparable." Such a belief relates closely to Lao Tsu's words that opposites "find their completion only through each other." Kurtz states that "the common denominator in all my managers is that they are professional risk-takers, as you can't have investment rewards without it." He adds, "Those that know how to take and live with risk are the winners in the investment game." Don is no stranger to risk-taking. He took many gutsy positions in the days when he personally supervised Equitable's investment portfolio decisions. In the early 1970s, before the phrase "nifty fifty" was coined, Don was offered and purchased a very large block of Disney from a large New York City bank, as well as an equally large position in American Express from one of the largest and best-known mutual funds. Though the stakes were very large, Kurtz believed, and Equitable's portfolios benefited.

Don advises individual investors to stick to investments that are in areas that they know and understand. He also feels that it is important to have access to good information sources and to have people whom you can bounce ideas off and who will tell you whether these ideas make sense or seem crazy.

Whether one is a professional or individual investor, Kurtz feels that the hardest thing to do is to keep in step with the market. Once out of step, it can be very difficult to get back, especially as one can easily press by trying too hard—like a baseball player in a hitting slump. Since one can easily make mistakes when pressing, Kurtz advises that one should occasionally put his hands in his pockets and walk away from the market action for a while. Sounding a bit like Lao Tsu, Don adds, "It is important to stay relaxed, calm, and low-key so that when one has the clarity to see daylight, then one can move decisively. That is good risk-taking."

CHARWOMAN INVESTING

Grand Dame Muriel Lucas was left a tidy sum when her husband, a British general, suddenly passed away. When her solicitor and banker met with her to recommend how her affairs should be handled, they were shocked when she announced that she intended to handle her own investments.

Several years later the same advisers, amazed at her outstanding investment success, sought out Mrs. Lucas to discover the reason why. Mrs. Lucas told them that she couldn't have done it without her charwoman (cleaning lady). Over tea, the Grand Dame would talk to her charwoman to discover what she and her friends were doing, buying, etc. Mrs. Lucas then invested in those companies that benefited from her charwoman's patronage.

The author's two best investment successes actually occurred before he went to Wall Street. After being discharged from the Army in 1961 at the age of twenty-four, he flew from St. Louis to Chicago in one of the early jets, a Boeing 707. In the air, he became excited about the plane's speed, comfort, and quietness. Upon landing, he spoke to the pilot, who was saying good-bye to the passengers. Congratulating him on having such a fine airplane, the author added that it was too bad that such a luxurious plane must be incredibly expensive to operate. The pilot took issue, pointing out that jets were actually much cheaper to operate than piston aircraft because they had fewer moving parts. The next week the author, excited over better and cheaper airplanes, purchased what for him were serious positions in Northwest and United Airlines—a move that was rewarded with a tenfold profit.

Three years later, after receiving an MBA, the author began working for the Gallo Wine Company. Reviewing trends in wine sales, he noticed that, though overall wine consumption was declining slightly, table wines were growing 10 percent per year and champagne was growing at a remarkable 25 percent rate. Noting that the Taylor Wine Company of Hammonsport, N.Y., was not only one of the few publicly traded wine companies (it is now a subsidiary of Coke), but also the largest domestic producer of champagne, the author asked Ernest Gallo, a tough cookie with a critical eye, what he thought of Taylor. When Ernest said it was a good company, the author needed no additional research and again bought heavily (this one tripled).

Thousands of times every day Americans are investing in ideas that come from their own observations of the world around them, whether it be from personal or work-related experience. Likewise, Jim Rogers, Roy Neuberger, Don Kurtz, and Dame Muriel Lucas have all realized their best investments through observing the nature of things and by following a few simple disciplines. As long as the author did the same, he also had excellent results. Unfortunately, when he "turned pro" by going to Wall Street, his investment results often turned sour. The problem was that he too often focused on the trees, rather than the forest. By getting fancy and following the artificial rules of security analysis, the author often ended up playing a loser's game.

Investment success does not belong to those with the "magic formula," but to those with the courage of their own wisdom.

Drawing by Richard Decker; © 1957 The New Yorker Magazine, Inc.

"To hell with a balanced portfolio. I want you to sell my Fenwick Chemical and sell it <u>now</u>."

10

THE YIN AND YANG

*Know the male, but keep the
female.*
—LAO TSU

*The market is like a beautiful
woman—endlessly fascinat-
ing, endlessly complex, always changing, always mystifying.*
—EDWARD C. JOHNSON, JR.
Fidelity Management

A loan officer of a large bank took notice when his wife
mentioned that she had been shopping at W. T. Grant's and
would never shop there again. Since his bank had a large
loan outstanding to Grant's, he asked her why she would
not return. She replied that the salesclerks had made her
uncomfortable as they kept following her around. When he
said that should not happen since Grant's is a self-service
store, his wife replied that the service people must have
been bored because there was almost no one in the store.

Concerned, the next morning the banker sought out the

loan officer in charge of tracking Grant's progress and asked if there was a problem. His fellow officer pulled out a spread sheet and pointed out that though overall sales were down slightly, sales per square foot were improving, and therefore there was no reason to be concerned. The outcome is now history, as Grant's became one of the largest bankruptcy cases in the country's history.

"Intuition is put down as mere 'women's intuition,'" states Dr. Jean Bolen, author of *The Tao of Psychiatry*. She adds that, "Reacting to a situation on a feeling level is drummed out of little boys, who are urged to be logical at all times." Aren't we all used to hearing youngsters challenging each other by declaring, "Oh, yeah, prove it!" Such societal preconditioning, fostered by our educational system, reinforces the scientific method, whereby if something can't be tested, proven, or otherwise measured, it is considered unimportant. Unfortunately, when change occurs, as it so often does in our dynamic world, it cannot be measured until after the fact. As a result the "world's smartest man" often ends up playing a loser's game by reacting to newness only when it is too late.

In the W. T. Grant's story, the male (yang) took the female's (yin) sensing seriously. His fault lay in then relying on the expert's measurement system to judge reality. He would have been better off sending some colleagues to the stores to see what was happening.

At a cocktail party, a husband pointed out to his small conversational circle that the bald man across the room was one of the world's most famous brain surgeons. "If I needed brain surgery, I would insist that he perform the operation," the man declared. "He's the best." His wife, in another conversation, also pointed out the renowned doctor: "I noticed at our club last week that the famous doctor spilled his coffee because his hand was shaking so badly. He would be the last person I would want to have operate on me."

In this case, the brain surgeon's credentials were impeccable and that was all the male needed to know. His wife, however, directly observed reality (the shaky hand) and sensed that something was wrong (the doctor, indeed, had suffered a minor stroke).

We continue to honor yang values by demanding credentials of anyone who asks us to look at what is new, rather than looking at the evidence itself. However, in times of accelerating change, the experts who use analytic tools are employing yang methods that are proving ineffective in sensing new directions.

It is the "Lao Tsu" right brain that can sense changing situations by using its yin feminine feeling, seeing, and sensing qualities. Unfortunately, the right brain operates at a disadvantage because it does not have the ability to communicate by speech. As George Bernard Shaw once quipped, "I have naught but a woman's reason: I think it's so because I think it's so."

One might say that the right brain suffers from the "Cassandra syndrome." According to Greek legend, Cassandra received an ironic punishment. Because she had lied, the gods condemned her to tell only the truth. She was given the ability to prophesy the future with unfailing accuracy, only never to be believed by those who heard her.

The right brain, like Cassandra, has an uncanny ability to sense reality. However, since it cannot communicate with yanglike language and also has little scientific status in our culture, it is usually put down as unimportant. Though knowledge, cleverness, and skepticism often prevail, these modes of thinking just as often fail us as they lack the appropriate sensitivity needed to perceive new trends.

THE MALE AND THE FEMALE MIND

Physiologically the minds of males and females are different. These differences, however, cannot be categorized in terms of hemispheric dominance (women are not more right brained than men or vice versa). Rather the difference is one of specialized (yang) versus generalized (yin) thinking. As a result, men tend to perform better as experts, whereas women tend to have an inherent superiority to see the gestalt, the big picture.

Male and female differences have been researched by Doctors Dianne McGinness and Karl Pribram of Stanford University. They found that males are more likely to excel at spatial relations, which are typical of the right hemisphere. They are more sensitive to cold than females, but less sensitive to heat. They have better daylight vision, but tend to see less well at night. Males also tend to be more interested in objects than in people, even though they tend to be more curious than females.

Females tend to be better in left-hemispheric verbal thoughts. They have better skin sensitivity (especially at the fingertips), hear better (especially at high ranges), sing in better tune, and have a more accurate sense of taste. They are also more attentive to people and tend to be better at social interaction as they have better verbal skills. The female often surpasses the male in tasks involving manual dexterity, fine coordination, and rapid choice.

Such biological differences between the sexes may in large part be related to their rates of maturation, in that girls mature much faster than boys. At birth, for example, girls are physiologically four weeks more developed than boys and reach puberty and maximum growth a full two to three years before males. Thus, girls begin to talk and read earlier than boys, and are much less likely (by a four-to-one margin) to have learning disabilities than males.

Because of early maturation, the two brain hemispheres in girls begin to interact earlier than in boys. Thus, the woman's earlier ability to involve both hemispheres simultaneously in a task gives them an advantage in seeing the whole. The male, on the other hand, since his two hemispheres operate independently for a longer time, tends to excel at specialized tasks (Einstein didn't talk in sentences until he was three). In his book *The Right Brain*, Thomas Blakeslee even goes so far as to hypothesize that there have not yet been any towering geniuses among women because of the inherent generalized nature of their thinking caused by their early maturation.

THE YANG OF IT

Someone once said that "if the only tool that man had was a hammer, he would treat everything as if it were a nail." As it has turned out, the only tool many experts use is the computer, so they tend to act as if the only things that count are those that can be computerized.

Even before the advent of the computer, man had begun to specialize through the development of expertise. As Francis Bacon said years ago, "Knowledge is power." But power can corrupt, and experts are known to use knowledge frequently as a putdown ("you don't have the facts, but I do").

The computer, as an extension of the brain's sequential and logical left hemisphere, has enhanced the imbalanced thinking of specialists. Furthermore, out of a fear of irrational and noncomputerizable elements, the computer has proved to be a great defense mechanism. It is interesting that although mankind has built machines that can not only duplicate left-brained thinking but do it millions of times faster and with greater accuracy, we have yet to devise machinery that can perform right-hemispheric reasoning. Consider, for example, that a baby can easily beat computers at facial recognition!

Analexic compulsion (where man tries to make everything measurable) compels computer experts to try to overpower the dark by making fixity out of flux. As Lao Tsu stated, "When knowledge becomes highly abstract, men are deceived by mistaking abstraction for reality." By extending the childhood taunt, "Oh, yeah, prove it," Americans instinctively play the role of the male. Often this results in business spending more time keeping records of what is being done than in doing business.

As "future shock" results in a world characterized by dynamic change, the expert and his computer become more and more obsolete as predictive tools. We simply can no longer afford to translate the world into linear form. Moreover, since the computer can only record known information, it is forced to ignore the unknown.

To change our thinking from reliance on yang qualities will not be easy. We must take courage in the words of Pablo Picasso: "Every act of creation first of all is an act of destruction, because the new idea will destroy what a lot of people believe is essential to the survival of their intellectual world."

WHAT'S BEING SAID, AND WHAT'S BEING DONE

If expertise is becoming less capable of handling a changing world, how are our business managers adapting? As discussed in chapter 3, Dr. Henry Mintzberg of McGill University has looked into the question of how top managers in the corporate world are actually operating. After observing several executives at work, Dr. Mintzberg concluded that they did not operate in the scientific manner espoused by our prestigious graduate business schools. Rather, he discovered that executive decision-makers showed a dislike for written communications and for long, step-by-step tasks. Moreover, they tended to pay scant attention to the computer runs in their in boxes (in boxes were not "in"). They thrived on disorder, ambiguity, and frequent interruptions. In short, he discovered that they clearly tended to be right-brained types with an appreciation for yin sensing.

The fact that top managers often ignore the analytic research of their staffs and depend on yin-type information such as gossip, hearsay, and speculation must come as quite a shock to MBAs who are trained in systematic thinking. Though the bureaucrats are making serious inroads into corporate America, business continues to be an art form that is disguised as a science—so that businessmen cannot be accused of making intuitive and emotional decisions.

IN SEARCH OF OUR MISSING INNER HALF

"It is because we single out something and treat it as distinct from other things that we get the idea of its opposite. Beauty, for example, once distinguished, suggests its opposite, ugliness...in fact, all distinctions naturally appear as opposites. And opposites get their meaning from each other and find their completion only through each other."

Lao Tsu's sense of polarity, as expressed above, certainly applies to the yin and the yang. Not only do we all possess both qualities, but we also complete a yin and yang coupling through marriage. By observing many marriages, it is the author's belief that we tend to marry our missing inner self. In terms of the brain hemispheres, in mating we tend to couple with someone of opposite brain dominance, so that left-brained types tend to mate with right-brainers. As Chinese physicians often say, the equilibrium of the yin and yang principles results in great longevity. Likewise, when a partner of a lifelong marriage dies, the other's life expectancy becomes greatly reduced. If the above hypothesis is valid (and it is a tentative one), there are many interesting implications, including why married couples so often have communication problems.

The possibility that we often marry our missing inner half also has an important implication for investment decision-making—namely, that one can be more "whole brained" by involving one's spouse in the decision-making process. Maybe your wife/husband isn't interested in facts or figures, but she/he might be a keen observer of the real world (the one that stocks sooner or later must respond to). Had our friend from Houston who lost 75 percent of his portfolio of energy stocks in just one year been married, his wife might have pointed out how people were purchasing more sweaters and were turning down their thermostats to conserve energy. Remember, our brain dominance tends to hold the key to both our strengths and our weaknesses.

THE STOCK MARKET AS A FEMALE

"The market is like a beautiful woman—endlessly fascinating, endlessly complex, always changing, always mystifying." So states Edward C. Johnson, Jr., of Fidelity Management, whom many consider to be the modern dean of Wall Street. Furthermore, as we saw earlier, Mr. Johnson strongly believes that investing is not a science, but rather an art form.

As was mentioned in Chapter 1, the stock market's dynamics are very much related to crowd behavior. As Gustave Le Bon states in *The Crowd*, "A crowd has the mind of a single woman." Despite the market's obvious yin characteristics of uncertainty and flux, Wall Street professionals continue to treat it with yang principles. By applying logic to the illogical, Wall Street continues to play a loser's game, as is seen by the fact that fewer than one in three outperform the averages.

Besides using the wrong tool for the task, (i.e., the left hemisphere to understand yinlike flux), the yang quality of competition is a dominating aspect of the professional investment arena on Wall Street. For instance, the analytic community competes in order to determine which analysts are voted to the *Institutional Investor*'s All-Star Research Team. And unfortunately, the votes tend to be cast more for those who have detailed knowledge than for those with wisdom.

Wall Street analysts also love to proclaim that one company has good management but another does not. How do Wall Street analysts know good from bad? That's a good question, as few of them have ever managed anything themselves. Moreover, since Wall Street firms are notorious for their own poor management practices, analysts do not exactly have a good role model to choose from. In reality, "good management" means that the company has done well in the past, leaving money managers the task of figuring out whether the success should be credited to the horse or the jockey.

Investment money managers also compete. Since the managers of mutual funds have their portfolios quoted daily in the paper, they tend to compare the results of their fund with those of the competition. And doing better than the competition is the name of the game, since it influences which fund the public is going to buy. One of the side effects of such competition is the "winner's syndrome," which occurs when one actually does vault into first place. Once there, one then tends to look back over his shoulder to watch what the competition is doing. This can be very hazardous to your vision.

Pension fund managers also compete, as they try to outperform each other so as to be ranked in the top quartile in the Becker Survey. Moreover, since their portfolios are reviewed quarterly, money managers commonly do some "window dressing." Window dressing refers to the process whereby money managers near the end of the quarter sell the stocks that performed badly and buy the ones that did best. Though it makes their portfolio "look better," it often affects performance negatively. Everyone rushes to one side of the ship (i.e., buys the same stocks) to the point where the stocks become top-heavy and capsize.

The pension fund administrators of corporations also merrily contribute to the competitive process. It works like this: Company XYZ has seven money managers for its pension fund. Every two years they fire the two managers with the worst performance record and hire two new managers who have had outstanding records over the last few years. Sounds good? Yes, but in reality it is just another loser's game. The managers who were fired most likely owned stocks that were out of phase with the market. Since the market changes about every two years as industry group strength rotates (i.e., growth stocks will do well for a while and then fade as cyclicals or energy stocks, etc. become hot), the firings will get rid of the managers whose stock may be

From *The Wall Street Journal*; permission — Cartoon Features Syndicate

"The true meaning of life? Sure, just a second. . . ."

just about to come back into favor. Conversely, the new managers are likely to be heavily positioned in the groups that, though they have done well, may be ready to peak out. Therefore, it might be wiser for Company XYZ to fire the two best performers and hire two new ones who have had abysmal performance records!

Alan Watts stated, "The art of life is not seen as holding the yang and banishing the yin, but as keeping the two in balance, because there cannot be one without the other." The poor performance by most professional Wall Street investors is the result of an imbalance of the yin and the yang, a lack of whole-brainedness.

The left-brained analytic system on Wall Street has become overdeveloped. Like a tree that has grown too large for its place in the forest, it has crowded out intuition, vision, creativity, and gestalt sensing, which are the properties of the right hemisphere. As professionals of the Street continue to try to overpower darkness, opportunities will exist for those who can sense new directions.

11

THE UNCARVED BLOCK

Everything has an original simplicity, power, beauty, and magnificence. Unfortunately, such natural qualities are easily spoiled and lost when that simplicity is changed. By following the artificial rules of man, one can easily ignore the inner potential of his uncarved block. The uncarved block is the natural simplicity of everything—whether it be a block of wood or a person.

Moses and Jesus were playing golf. On a three-par hole where the drive carried mostly across the water, Jesus hit his drive into the middle of the pond. When Moses asked what club he had used, Jesus replied, "A seven iron, just like Jack Nicklaus always uses on this hole." Moses shook his head and said, "That's the wrong club, you should use a four." After Moses parted the water and returned the ball to Jesus, Jesus got set to hit it again when Moses asked, "What club are you using this time?" Jesus replied, "A seven, just like Nicklaus," and promptly put his second drive into the far side of the pond.

Again Moses parted the water and retrieved the ball. Again he told Jesus he was using the wrong club. Again Jesus said that it was the right club because Jack Nicklaus always used it and added that he just hadn't hit it correctly. "OK," said Moses, "but this time if it goes into the water, I'm not going to get it." Jesus took a mighty swing and the ball did clear the pond, only to hit the far bank and roll back into the water. As Jesus was walking across the water to get the ball, a foursome of golfers came up to the tee. One startled player asked Moses about his water-walking playing partner. "Who does he think he is, Jesus Christ?" "No," Moses replied, "he thinks he's Jack Nicklaus!"

As Adam Smith, author of *The Money Game*, states, "If you don't know who you are, the stock market is an expensive place to find out." Just as a fish can't whistle, a lot of us blindly do what we aren't designed to do; we ignore the potentials of our uncarved block. Often we select a particular career because we are told it's the thing to do. Then society plays a cruel joke; it allows us to be successful enough to make a living, and at the same time locks us into a lifestyle that we can't afford to give up. Similarly, by not correctly distinguishing the genuine from the artificial, investment errors are likely to follow.

Such forms of self-deception can be the products of

"hemispheric ignorance." By being unaware of which mode of thought dominates our judgments, we often rely on analytic processes when intuitive sensing would be more appropriate (or vice versa). We tend to use the wrong tool for the task.

THE HERRMANN INDICATOR

All of us prefer one hemisphere over the other when we make investment decisions. Though such a preference may be slight for some of us, in other cases the difference can be pronounced. In addition, we tend to operate in either a lower (limbic) or upper (cerebral) mode. The Herrmann Brain Dominance Indicator is designed to indicate your preference; this, in turn, can help you determine how to achieve more complete, whole-brained judgments.

Instructions: Based on your own self-assessment, rate yourself on each statement from a low of zero to a high of 25 points. Be as objective as you can in determining your rating. Be discriminating in your self-assessment. Do not give yourself points without merit. Do not hold back points that you do merit.

1. It is important to personally analyze the performance of companies whose stocks I am considering for an investment   _____

2. Keeping detailed records of all my stock transactions improves the quality of my investment decisions   _____

3. Frequently the best market input is "gut feel"   _____

4. I pride myself on having a real "sense" of the market _____

5. I base my investment decisions on historic correlations _____

6. A key to investment success is careful planning _____

7. It is the personalities of the corporate leaders that I pay close attention to _____

8. As far as I am concerned, intuition is just as, if not more important, than factual data _____

9. For me, it is facts and numbers and how they add up that count _____

10. You don't know whom to trust in this business _____

11. I can't explain my stock picks; they just feel right _____

12. I like to be spontaneous about my investment decisions _____

13. I want all the input I can get, there is never enough data _____

14. Certain disciplines are absolutely basic to investment success _____

15. For me, the market is a live, living thing _____

16. I can frequently anticipate the results of my investment decisions _____

17. In this crazy investment world, there is only one way to win and that is to be as rational as possible _____

18. To me, organization is the key. Good organization and success go hand in hand _____

19. Sometimes the reactions of my body
    tell me the direction to go _____
20. There is a rhythm and pattern to the
    market that I can sense and rely on _____

SCORING:

Fill in the score for each of the twenty questions in the appropriate group below, and then total:

CEREBRAL LEFT		CEREBRAL RIGHT	
Question #1	_____	4	_____
5	_____	8	_____
9	_____	12	_____
13	_____	16	_____
17	_____	20	_____
Total	_____	Total	_____
Points	_____*	Points	_____*

LIMBIC LEFT		LIMBIC RIGHT	
2	_____	3	_____
6	_____	7	_____
10	_____	11	_____
14	_____	15	_____
18	_____	19	_____
Total	_____	Total	_____
Points	_____*	Points	_____*
Total Left	_____	Total Right	_____
Percent Left	_____	Percent Right	_____

---

*NOTE: 1, 2, or 3 points are given depending on the total score for the subcategory. A total of 0 to 33 is given 3 points; 34 to 66, 2 points; and 67 or higher is awarded 1 point. Place the points in the appropriate space in the circular diagram below.

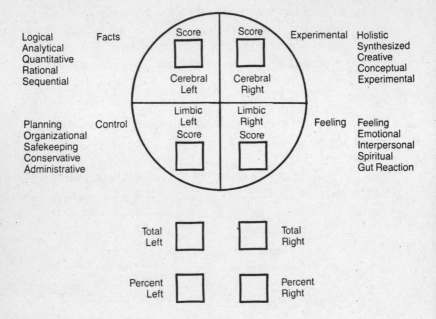

INTERPRETATION—THE HERRMANN INDICATOR·

If you scored evenly in all four quadrants, you are a balanced investor—a good sign. Keep investing, but be careful to maintain the balance. Be sure not to rely too much on other people who operate heavily in just one or two modes. If you are evenly balanced and score mainly in the "1" category, you have good company, as that is the profile of most corporate CEOs.

If you score heavily on either the left or right side, then you have a hemispheric imbalance. Knowing your bias can turn a weakness into a strength, as you should do well those things that fit your preference. To achieve whole-brainedness in investing, however, you need to offset your bias by interacting with others who have a complementary dominance (see later part of chapter).

Catty-corner dominance of cerebral left and limbic right (facts/feelings) or of limbic left and cerebral right (experimental/control) is the most difficult profile for successful investing. Herrmann's research indicates that individuals with such profiles tend to be inconsistent in which mode they use. Rather than their brain halves complementing each other, they tend to compete; one side can gain only at the expense of the other (i.e., you can't be experimental and in control at the same time, or simultaneously logical and emotional).

Because experimental/control functions cannot occur at the same time, investors with such profiles will oscillate between modes. For example, if the experimental mode dominates a decision that proves to be wrong, the control mode will have a greater say next time around. If, on the other hand, the risk-taking by the experimental mode pays off, chances are the experimental mode will take even more risk. If left unchecked, risk-taking can snowball out of control. The way to offset this "catty-corner (experimental/control) syndrome" is to employ more facts and feelings (i.e., the opposite quadrants) either directly or through consulting with someone who operates in those modes.

In the same way, one with a tendency to facts/feelings, cerebral left and limbic right, will also have oscillation problems. In addition, he is apt to become overly enthusiastic about someone who has all the facts and figures and make the mistake of betting on the "world's smartest man." As a result, he may end up without a financial parachute.

TAO INVESTORS

When I interviewed Don Kurtz, I became somewhat concerned when he said that he staffed his organization with people who think the way he does. The concern disappeared when I saw Kurtz's score on the Herrmann Brain Dominance Indicator. He is very much a whole-brained investor (see below) and thus has striven to build a whole-brained organization.

	PERCENT LEFT	PERCENT RIGHT	UPPER LEFT	LOWER LEFT	UPPER RIGHT	LOWER RIGHT
	TAO INVESTORS—HERRMANN SCORES					
Jim Rogers	66%	34%	1	1	2	2
Roy Neuberger	45	55	1	2	1	1
Don Kurtz	48	52	1	1	1	1
Ben Goodspeed	36	64	2	2	1	1

Like Kurtz, Roy Neuberger appears to be quite whole brained, though he does show a slight preference for using the right brain. Jim Rogers, on the other hand, values the discipline of the left brain in his investment decisions. The author prefers to rely most heavily on his right brain. This may well explain his tendency to become emotionally attached to his stocks, which results in sometimes overstaying positions (i.e., holding stocks too long). All four of the subjects scored numerically high (at the one or two level), much more so than is typical.

THE $64,000 QUESTION

In the popular quiz show of the 1950s, "The $64,000 Question," contestants were placed in an isolation booth and asked questions with ascending degrees of difficulty. If one achieved a certain level, he or she was allowed to bring an expert of their choice into the booth for help. Investing is like "The $64,000 Question," in that we are allowed to employ experts to help us find the answers. However, in investing one also has to develop the questions, a task where experts are not skilled. In effect, investing is often a two-part function. Feelings tend to precede logic, so that the intuitive, right side often develops the questions while the left supplies the answers. Our right brain serves as an inner compass by providing an amazing instinct for the right direction, while the left knows normality, facts, figures, probabilities, etc. As we saw in Wallas's creativity model depicted in Chapter 5, successful decision-making is a product of the proper interaction of both brains. And, as Lao Tsu adds, "When opposites supplement each other, everything is harmonious."

Knowing one's dominant hemisphere should serve as a confidence builder for investing. If you are left brained, logically dominated, you should have the confidence that you can develop investment skills by learning more about the logical elements of the investment game. Conversely, an intuitive right-brainer should learn to trust his or her instincts and judgments. Such confidence can help avoid the trap Lao Tsu worried about when he stated, "Because people have little respect for themselves, they are easily influenced by each other."

Weakness can do you a big favor, if you acknowledge that it's there. Knowing your brain dominance can be invaluable in understanding your missing inner half. Since we tend unconsciously to select evidence that will support our point of view, we have to avoid too much reliance on others who have similar brain profiles as ourselves. If one is logical, he or she should look to team up with others who are intuitively dominated, and vice versa. Often, one has to look no farther than their spouse for such a complement.

When making investment decisions, it is advisable to stop and ask which side of your brain is running with the ball. Have you thought about logical considerations? Does it feel right? When your gut says one thing, does your logic say another? If so, it is best to defer judgment; chances are that your hemispheres are in disagreement. If you learn to give each brain equal voting power, you will have a constitutional balance of power as each mode of thinking has the power to temper the other. As the two sides interact in a balanced way, they can then synergistically build upon the value added by the other half's contribution.

The ability to defer judgment is a quality that creative thinkers possess, according to many studies. The resistance to "premature closure," as it is dubbed, is the phenomenon in which an individual does not rush in to develop a point of view, but rather is content to "wait and see." Both Roy Neuberger and Don Kurtz recommend investor patience, and Jim Rogers achieved his portfolio increase by using only a relatively few major insights.

Left-brained, logical investors need to observe the law of reverse effort. When a decision seems so perfect that it

can't miss, one should take a walk or "sleep on it" in order
to give the right brain an opportunity to participate in the
decision. Your right brain will work on your investing even
when it is out of your left mind. It will, in effect, be working
while you sleep. For this reason, many people keep pen and
notepaper at their bedside table, to harvest compelling ideas
that pop up at night.

YAQUI INVESTING

Carlos Castaneda, in his book *The Teachings of Don Juan:
A Yaqui Way of Knowledge*, outlines Don Juan's description of
the four enemies one must overcome to become a "man of
knowledge," or in this case a wise investor.

The first enemy is fear. If a man runs away out of fear
and avoids investing, nothing will happen except that he
will never learn. Though you can read many books about
the theory of investing, you can never learn unless you
become a player. The different investment techniques such
as options, short sales, bonds, etc. also can be known only
through doing, as that is how you can best acquire a feel.

Fear is overcome by clarity, which then becomes an investor's second enemy. Clarity of mind about the investment process, which is hard to obtain, dispels fears, but it
also blinds. It forces you not to doubt yourself and gives you
the false assurance that you can do anything you please, for
you see clearly into everything. If you yield to this power,
which is only a point before your eyes, you have succumbed
to your second enemy. Remember, in analysis what can get
you into trouble is not what you took into account, but
rather the variables you never questioned. You must use
your clarity and use it only to see, and wait patiently and

measure carefully before taking the next step. You must understand above all that your clarity is almost an illusion. In investing, it is dangerous to feel too secure.

One who overcomes clarity possesses power, but this too is an enemy. One who is defeated by this third enemy, power, dies without really knowing how to handle it. To conquer power, you have to defy it deliberately. You have to realize that the power you have seemingly conquered when your investments succeed was never really yours. You must keep everything in check and know how to use your power. For Lao Tsu, power means understanding ''the way of the universe.'' If you do not possess such understanding, power can come and go, as the highly publicized technician Joe Granville has found out. If you have such power, it should be used only when it feels right and not viewed as anointing you as an "investor for all seasons."

The fourth enemy to becoming a wise investor is old age, where you must resist the unyielding desire to rest. In investing, old age does not relate to physical age, as Roy Neuberger has convincingly demonstrated. Rather, it relates to a tiring concentration where you stop questioning the changing world or stop following a holding under the excuse that "it has gone up so much I can't afford to sell it because of the capital gains tax." It is dangerous to give in to "old age" because you always have to be looking in order to maintain power over your investment portfolio in a changing world.

THE ARTICULATE INCOMPETENT

If you choose not to seek investment power, then you can always (provided you have a minimum of $100,000 to invest) give the power for a fee to a professional investment adviser. Lesser amounts can be given to a stockbroker on a "discretionary basis." In so doing, you not only should be careful about whom you select, but also should monitor the performance wisely, as power given can be power taken away.

As Robert Bernstein, the chairman of Random House, said, "In business, only intuition can protect you against the most dangerous individual of all—the articulate incompetent." Since investment counseling seems to have more than its share of "articulate incompetents," the following guidelines may prove helpful:

1. Insist on meeting with the individual who will be managing your account. It is often his judgment that will be the key ingredient in what happens to your portfolio, since in most investment organizations, investment recommendations are suggestions that the staff may or may not follow. This person's judgment is the main thing you are paying for.

2. Ask what role personal judgment plays in the individual's decisions, as well as the firm's overall investment philosophy. Avoid those who use investment strategies that rely too heavily on mechanical methodology.

3. Avoid "investment scholars." If an investment counselor is too articulate, if he creates a barrier of words you can't understand, be careful. Conversely, if he or she is not unduly articulate and uses feeling and sensing words, look at this tendency as one indication of right-brained thinking.

4. Be sure your account is meaningful to the investment manager. If your account is small, find a small-size manage-

BROO... HILDA

Intellect
vs.
Intuition

ROUND
ONE

DEFINITIONS:

Intellect: COLLECTION
OF LEARNED FACTS.
NO GUARANTEE OF
RELEVANCY.

Intuition: INSPIRATION
AND PERCEPTION SPRING-
ING FROM UNLIMITED
RESERVOIR OF INNER
TRUTH.

Intellect:
DON'T CROSS.
EACH YEAR
THOUSANDS
DIE IN TRAFFIC
ACCIDENTS.

Intellect:
CHARACTER
DISORDER RESULTING
IN CHRONIC
IRRITABILITY.

Intuition:
DUCK!

ZA...

ment firm or your money will become only an account number on a computer printout. Big is not necessarily beautiful; having a large research staff not only does not guarantee good investment judgments, it often serves as a poor substitute.

5. Ask what mistakes the investment adviser and his firm have made. There is an ancient Chinese saying, "One disease, long life; no disease, short life." If a person has had a disease, a warning, then he will take care of himself and increase the odds of living a long life. Likewise, if an investment adviser has not yet made major errors, be careful, as he or she is probably getting close to perfecting the art of going wrong with confidence—something you do not want someone to do with your money.

6. Don't be overly impressed with investment firms that have had highly successful investment performance records within the recent past. You might be giving money to an organization that is so happily riding the last trend that they will be the last to admit when the trend is ending.

7. If your investment adviser plays golf, ask him what his handicap is. If it is under six, be careful; the chances are he is either lying or spending far too much time on the golf course.

8. Try to determine how whole brained the investment adviser's philosophy and procedures are. Over the long run, balanced investing is the best investing.

9. Once you select an investment adviser, give him a fair chance. For the first five years the Dallas football franchise, under Coach Tom Landry, had losing seasons. Upset about negative fan reaction, one club official approached owner Clint Murchison about the unrest of the fans. Clint

told the official to give Coach Landry a ten-year contract, as that should keep the fans quiet.

THE TAO OF POOH

Under many circumstances it makes sense to have an investment adviser. However, one should never choose one solely because "I couldn't possibly do as well as a professional." Remember the statistics? Only 32 out of 100 of the pros will outperform the market averages if they hold true to historic norms. Don't forget that the intuitive qualities of your right hemisphere can do incredible things, if you give them the opportunity. The chances are good that you can beat the professionals and have fun doing it.

Benjamin Hoff in his marvelous book *The Tao of Pooh* points out that "the masters of life know the Way. They listen to the voice within them, the voice of wisdom and simplicity, the voice that reasons beyond cleverness and knows beyond knowledge. That voice is not just the power and property of a few, but has been given to everyone. It is the key to harnessing the power of the uncarved block."

THE INVESTMENT ALPHABET

The power of intuitive understanding will protect you from harm until the end of your days.
—LAO TSU

In business, only intuition can protect you against the most dangerous individual of all —the articulate incompetent.
—ROBERT BERNSTEIN,
Chairman, Random House

The Taoists tell a story of a farmer whose horse ran away. Because the horse was a prize mare, the neighbors stopped by to express their condolences, to which the farmer said, "Perhaps." The next week the horse returned, bringing with her five wild horses. When the neighbors stopped in to congratulate the farmer on his good luck, he answered, "Perhaps." The next day, when the farmer's son was trying to ride one of the wild horses, he fell off and broke his leg. Again the neighbors gathered to express their sympathy for the farmer's misfortune. Again the farmer said, "Perhaps."

Three days later, army conscription officers rode into the village and seized all of the young men except the farmer's son, who was rejected because of his broken leg. When the neighbors came by to say how fortunate it was that everything had worked out, the farmer said, "Perhaps."

As Lao Tsu wrote, "Nature alternates dynamically," and so the stock market alternates in a cycle of fortune and misfortune. As crisis is comprised of danger and opportunity, those who sense change in the early stages will tend to have the most bountiful harvest. This sensitivity is such a key part of the investment game that most of us feel it is a skill only someone else could possess. This phenomenon has led to the development of the "guru syndrome."

The guru syndrome is the notion that the Wall Street professional who most convincingly predicts the last major stock market or interest rate move must have all the answers. Whether it be a Henry Kaufman, Joe Granville, or Stanley Berge, the predictor becomes the one everyone wants to follow. After investors walk in lockstep with the guru over the cliff, a new guru who pointed the way correctly (though only a few listened) is thrust to the forefront. When he too falls, investors will again fanatically search for a new guru so as to perpetuate the guru loser's game.

THE INVESTMENT ALPHABET

In the winner's game there is no magic formula for investment success. There is no guru with a magic cape whom you can follow with impunity. What exists is you and your uncarved block, complete with its remarkable intuitive inner compass.

What advice will work for you? Only you can decide

that. What I offer are selections for you to choose from. So feel free to take home from the Goodspeed Investment Alphabet whatever you feel comfortable about.

A. BE A LIGHT SLEEPER. Believe in the wisdom of insecurity; be a light sleeper. In our rapidly changing world it is important to be sensitive to changing conditions so as to recognize them before they are announced in the headlines or earnings reports. Remember, the difference between a comedy and a tragedy is that in a comedy the characters figure out reality in time to do something about it.

B. BE YOUR OWN JUDGE OF VALUE. Bargains are seldom announced, and those that are advertised as bargains often aren't. Be your own value assessor and resist being dissuaded by the "tent show barkers." As Lao Tsu wrote, "He who discriminates wisely avoids danger."

C. DO NOT BE TOO SURE. When you are the most certain that you are right, it is time to become the most nervous. Sure, you may be absolutely right—today. But tomorrow may be a different story, as the water flows the calmest just before the falls. As Alfred North Whitehead said, "It is the business of the future to be dangerous."

D. STAY DIVERSIFIED. Putting all your eggs in one basket can be very dangerous. This idea conjures up visions of a bird peering intently into its nest with its rear exposed to the world. The world is so dynamic, so interrelated, and so changeable that one has to watch the whole world to know what might next impact the basket. Stay diversified. As Lao Tsu warns, "Going to extremes is never best."

E. AVOID THE RECOMMENDATIONS OF EXPERTS. Avoid depending on well-known experts. Not only have they perfected the art of going wrong with confidence, but their advice is so widely disseminated as to give no one a real advantage. If you depend on the judgment of experts for investing, you have given your proxy to the "world's smartest man" and will all too often end up without a parachute. Don't forget, most experts are using only half a brain.

F. VALUE THE ART OF SELLING. The key to investment success is knowing when to sell, for as Lao Tsu pointed out, "Nature's brightest day fades into night." Since 90 percent of the Street's recommendations are on the buy side, there is little competition for selling advice. Selling is the highest art form of investing. "Finishing always triumphs over starting out," according to Lao Tsu. And he added, "People usually fail when they are on the verge of success, so give as much care to the end as the beginning. Then there will be no failure."

G. BE COMFORTABLE WITH RISK-TAKING. Investing and risk-taking are inseparable. In order to be a successful investor, one has to understand and accept risk. Regardless of what you may hear, all investments contain risk, to the point where the most dangerous investments are sometimes advertised as being the safest.

H. STICK TO WHAT YOU KNOW. Unless you can visualize something, you can't obtain it. Therefore, if you cannot understand a company's business or its purpose, avoid it. There are plenty of fish in the ocean. As in driving, don't invest beyond the range of your headlights.

I. USE VALUE GUIDELINES. Try to develop yardsticks for measuring value, whether it be market value (the stock's price times the number of shares outstanding), asset value, or price-earnings ratio (Roy Neuberger avoids stocks over 15 times earnings). This is one area where left-brained systematic thinking can serve as an invaluable check on right-hemispheric emotional enthusiasm.

J. TAKE YOUR LOSSES. Admit your mistakes and take your losses. As Roy Neuberger practices, take a loss whenever you lose 10 percent on an investments. Lao Tsu advised, "Take care of what is difficult while it is still easy." And, as Neuberger points out, "This creates a reserve of buying power that can be used to make fresh judgments."

K. DON'T PROCRASTINATE IN DECISION-MAKING. Avoid "jogging in place" with your portfolio. Failure to decide is, in effect, a decision. If you would not care to buy each holding in your portfolio each day, you should sell it (barring tax considerations).

L. DON'T CHURN YOUR ACCOUNT. Making money in the market is not like making bread; you don't knead the dough to make it rise. In-and-out trading is not only expensive, it also is dangerous to guess what current is going to sweep along the crowd. "In making furniture," Lao Tsu pointed out, "the more you carve the wood, the weaker it gets."

M. DON'T FIGHT THE TAPE. On a tombstone is inscribed, "Here lies John Day who died defending his right-of-way. He was dead right as he sped along, but now he's just as dead as if he were wrong." Moral of the story: Near-term, the "artificial rules of man" can prevail as in a fad. Such a trend may be wrong, but it is often wiser to wait for it to pass rather than fight it. Therefore, timing is an essential ingredient in investing, as waiting on the sidelines is often wiser than fighting the tape.

N. DON'T JUST HOPE. When Pandora opened her box,

out came fear, sin, pestilence, greed, and all the other ills that beset mankind. The last one to come from the box was hope. Hope is a false god, and can be an investor's greatest enemy. In investing, waiting for Santa Claus to bail you out can be costly. As Lao Tsu wrote, "When things reach maturity, they decay of themselves." Hope can interfere with seeing such realities.

O. AVOID INSIDER INFORMATION. As a "canny Scot" associated with one of the famous Scottish investment trusts stated, "Follow a tip from a company's president, and you will lose half your money. Get a tip from the chairman, and you will lose all of it."

P. WHEN YOU FEEL OUT OF SYNC, DON'T PLAY. When you don't feel in step with the market, walk away from it temporarily. If you push too hard, like a baseball player fighting a batting slump, you are likely to "mar the jade."

Q. AVOID FORMULA INVESTING. Over time, formula investing cannot work in a rapidly changing world. In a similar manner, one should not be heavily influenced by historic correlations. Just because the stock market went up 80 percent of the time after the Mets won a doubleheader doesn't mean it will go up the next time. Try not to confuse chance with cause and effect.

R. TRUST YOUR VISION. Use your eyes. Just as Jim Rogers spotted an investment opportunity when he saw women going to the natural look, so can you see dangers and opportunities by being alert to your personal and work environments. Without vision, investors will perish.

S. MISTAKES ARE OK. Don't be afraid to make mistakes. As Edward Johnson, Jr., of Fidelity Management points out,

"You learn by mistakes. When I look back, my life seems to be an endless chain of mistakes."

T. BE COMFORTABLE HOLDING CASH. Nothing in nature is as powerful as a void and that's why "cash" is so difficult to hold. However, one of the keynotes of creativity is to avoid "premature closure." Remember, as John Train likes to say, "Your broker, like a shark, will die if he isn't in motion." Thus, brokers (did you ever wonder why they are called "brokers?" Why not "brokest?") are not too keen to recommend cash positions.

U. USE BOTH BRAINS. Sleep on investment ideas. When an idea seems logical, when you find yourself in a "can't-miss" situation, it may be that your left brain has talked you into something that sounds good, but is fraught with danger. Take a walk or sleep on it in order to give your right brain equal time.

V. BOUNCE YOUR IDEAS. Find others with whom you can discuss your ideas, whether it be your spouse, a coworker, broker, or anyone else. If your "support system" is from someone of complementary brain dominance, your investing will be that much more well-rounded. Just make sure that you remain aloof enough to make the actual final judgment.

W. VIEW YOURSELF AS A TYPICAL CONSUMER. We in the Western world tend to focus on personal differences. In reality, human beings, regardless of their nationalities or backgrounds, are much more alike than they are different. Thus, what you are buying, saving, and feeling is much more a reflection of the "universal consumer" than most of us would care to admit. Your actions and those of your family should thus provide many profitable investment clues.

X. COINCIDENCE IS MORE THAN CHANCE. In Taoism, "the way of the universe" is an interconnected one. The concept of synchroneity—the idea that coincidence is more than just chance—can greatly heighten an investor's awareness. By looking at a "coincidence" as an event that contains a message, you can become sensitive to opportunities and dangers that otherwise you would likely ignore.

Y. AVOID THE PIED PIPER. Just because someone has been right seven times in a row is no guarantee that number eight will work out. When he is finally wrong, the size of the herd will be at its maximum—just as it plunges over the cliff and into the sea.

Z. BE PATIENT, BUT MOVE DECISIVELY. Use both your yin and yang qualities in investing. Sense the opportunities with yin qualities, and then seize the opportunities with yanglike decisiveness. Good investing is a matter of waiting to see the opening and then moving with strength. Lao Tsu wrote, "He who knows how to be aggressive, and yet remains patient, becomes a receptacle for all of Nature's lessons."

THE WARMTH OF THE HERD

Wall Street has a bias in favor of logical, left-brained thinking. Consequently, the right-brained sensing needed to decipher changing conditions tends to be ignored or overridden by reason. As a result, the collective wisdom is often surprised.

Happiness is running with the crowd, and Wall Street certainly is famous for its herd instinct. It is nice and cozy in the center of the herd, where the body heat is the greatest. However, there is danger in being too comfortable, as one is not at a good vantage point to observe the subtle early indicators of changing conditions. To be a successful investor over time, you need to become nervous when others start feeling secure. This is the "wisdom of insecurity."

True, it is difficult not to be swept up in herd thinking. People tend to mistrust mavericks who exercise independent thinking. Moreover, experts often act like sheepdogs, yipping at those who try to break free from the herd's "group think." To break free of the tyranny of the "world's smartest man," you need to learn to trust your intuitive right brain. Remember Lao Tsu's words, "The power of intuitive understanding will protect you from harm until the end of your days." Why? Because it is your intuitive understanding that will allow you to follow Lao Tsu's advice: "Take care of what is difficult while it is easy, and deal with what will become big while it is yet small."

All you need to accomplish this is to treat intuition as an equal partner with logic.

CREDITS
THE TAO JONES AVERAGES

STARRING
Lao Tsu

COSTARRING
Ned Herrmann

EDITED BY
Bill Whitehead and Rollin Stearns

PRODUCED BY INFERENTIAL FOCUS PARTNERS:
Andre Alkiewicz, Charlie Hess, Joe Kelly, and Peter Stehli

INTERVIEWEES:
Jim Rogers, Roy Neuberger, and Don Kurtz

DIRECTOR OF OFFICE LOGISTICS:
Fran Insinga

FEATURING:
The World's Smartest Man
The Articulate Incompetent

BASED ON THE WORKS OF
Tom Blakeslee   Dr. Joseph Bogen   Tony Buzan
Sir Arthur Conan Doyle   Dr. Betty Edwards   Albert Einstein
Charlie Ellis   Stewart Emery   Marilyn Ferguson
Tim Gallwey   Dr. Doug Heath   Ben Hoff
Dr. Henry Mintzberg   Trish Page   William Shakespeare
Adam Smith   Dr. Roger Sperry   John Train
Alan Watts   Holmes Welch

SPECIAL THANKS TO:

Mark Appleman   Bill Bullion   Bill Clayton
John Emmerling   Steve Gaber   Bob Goodspeed
Mike Grant   Pia Jorgenson   John Marshall
Eldon Mayer   Jim Osborn   Bob Perry
Chuck Royce   Ray Smith   Sandy Sulger
Ted Theodore   Des Towney   Jim Williams

WITH SPECIAL LOVE TO:
Toddy Goodspeed
Ben, Jr. and Mary Todd
Emily and Jonathan

FOR THE BEST IN PAPERBACKS, LOOK FOR THE

In every corner of the world, on every subject under the sun, Penguin represents quality and variety—the very best in publishing today.

For complete information about books available from Penguin—including Pelicans, Puffins, Peregrines, and Penguin Classics—and how to order them, write to us at the appropriate address below. Please note that for copyright reasons the selection of books varies from country to country.

In the United Kingdom: For a complete list of books available from Penguin in the U.K., please write to *Dept E.P., Penguin Books Ltd, Harmondsworth, Middlesex, UB7 0DA.*

In the United States: For a complete list of books available from Penguin in the U.S., please write to *Dept BA, Penguin*, Box 120, Bergenfield, New Jersey 07621-0120.

In Canada: For a complete list of books available from Penguin in Canada, please write to *Penguin Books Canada Ltd, 10 Alcorn Avenue, Suite 300, Toronto, Ontario, Canada M4V 3B2.*

In Australia: For a complete list of books available from Penguin in Australia, please write to the *Marketing Department, Penguin Books Ltd, P.O. Box 257, Ringwood, Victoria 3134.*

In New Zealand: For a complete list of books available from Penguin in New Zealand, please write to the *Marketing Department, Penguin Books (NZ) Ltd, Private Bag, Takapuna, Auckland 9.*

In India: For a complete list of books available from Penguin, please write to *Penguin Overseas Ltd, 706 Eros Apartments, 56 Nehru Place, New Delhi, 110019.*

In Holland: For a complete list of books available from Penguin in Holland, please write to *Penguin Books Nederland B.V., Postbus 195, NL-1380AD Weesp, Netherlands.*

In Germany: For a complete list of books available from Penguin, please write to *Penguin Books Ltd, Friedrichstrasse 10-12, D-6000 Frankfurt Main I, Federal Republic of Germany.*

In Spain: For a complete list of books available from Penguin in Spain, please write to *Longman, Penguin España, Calle San Nicolas 15, E-28013 Madrid, Spain.*

In Japan: For a complete list of books available from Penguin in Japan, please write to *Longman Penguin Japan Co Ltd, Yamaguchi Building, 2-12-9 Kanda Jimbocho, Chiyoda-Ku, Tokyo 101, Japan.*

☐ THE WOMEN OF BREWSTER PLACE
A Novel in Seven Stories
Gloria Naylor

Winner of the American Book Award, this is the story of seven survivors of an urban housing project — a blind alley feeding into a dead end. From a variety of backgrounds, they experience, fight against, and sometimes transcend the fate of black women in America today.

192 pages   ISBN: 0-14-006690-X

☐ STONES FOR IBARRA
Harriet Doerr

An American couple comes to the small Mexican village of Ibarra to reopen a copper mine, learning much about life and death from the deeply faithful villagers.   *214 pages   ISBN: 0-14-007562-3*

☐ WORLD'S END
T. Coraghessan Boyle

"Boyle has emerged as one of the most inventive and verbally exuberant writers of his generation," writes *The New York Times*. Here he tells the story of Walter Van Brunt, who collides with early American history while searching for his lost father.   *456 pages   ISBN: 0-14-009760-0*

☐ THE WHISPER OF THE RIVER
Ferrol Sams

The story of Porter Osborn, Jr., who, in 1938, leaves his rural Georgia home to face the world at Willingham University, *The Whisper of the River* is peppered with memorable characters and resonates with the details of place and time. Ferrol Sams's writing is regional fiction at its best.

528 pages   ISBN: 0-14-008387-1

☐ ENGLISH CREEK
Ivan Doig

Drawing on the same heritage he celebrated in *This House of Sky,* Ivan Doig creates a rich and varied tapestry of northern Montana and of our country in the late 1930s.   *338 pages   ISBN: 0-14-008442-8*

☐ THE YEAR OF SILENCE
Madison Smartt Bell

A penetrating look at the varied reactions to a young woman's suicide exactly one year later, *The Year of Silence* "captures vividly and poignantly the chancy dance of life." (*The New York Times Book Review*)

208 pages   ISBN: 0-14-011533-1

FOR THE BEST IN CONTEMPORARY AMERICAN FICTION